Vegan FOOD GIFTS

More Than 100 Inspired Recipes
for Homemade Baked Goods,
Preserves, and Other Edible Gifts
Everyone Will Love

JONI MARIE NEWMAN

Photography by Celine Steen and Illustrations by Kurt Halsey

FAIR WINDS
PRESS
BEVERLY, MASSACHUSETTS

© 2012 Fair Winds Press
Text © 2012 Joni Marie Newman

First published in the USA in 2012 by
Fair Winds Press, a member of
Quayside Publishing Group
100 Cummings Center
Suite 406-L
Beverly, MA 01915-6101
www.fairwindspress.com

16 15 14 13 12   1 2 3 4 5

ISBN: 978-1-59233-529-9

Digital edition published in 2012
eISBN: 978-1-61958-647-4

Library of Congress Cataloging-in-Publication Data

Newman, Joni-Marie.
Vegan food gifts : spread the vegan love diy-style with 100 inspired recipes for
homemade baked goods, preserves, and other edible gifts everyone will love / Joni
Marie Newman.
      p. cm.
 Includes index.
ISBN 978-1-59233-529-9
1. Vegan cooking. 2. Baking. I. Title.
TX837.N517 2012
641.5'636--dc23

                                                            2012020536

Cover design by Monica Rhines
Photography by Celine Steen, www.havecakewilltravel.com
Illustrations by Kurt Halsey, www.kurthalsey.com

Printed and bound in China

Dedication

This book is dedicated to the man who has stood by my side
through all sorts of craziness, heartbreak, sadness, and happiness.
We have grown up together since we were teenagers, and now as
"grown-ups" we have never loved each other more.

He, who always believed in me, even if he didn't always agree
with me—my husband, Dan. I love you.

Contents

Introduction

I have a confession to make. I wrote this book with a top-secret agenda. I plan to turn the whole world vegan … one gift at a time. What better way to show how fabulous and fun vegan foods can be than to give them away all wrapped up in pretty packages? After all, who can say no to a delicious peanut butter truffle or a package full of beautifully decorated cookies?

Besides turning the world vegan (no small task!), I also plan on furthering the DIY gift movement. When you make gifts yourself, you save the animals, you save the planet, and you say no to corporate greed, all in one fell swoop!

Whether you are an expert chef or a beginner cook, a crafty genius or someone without an artistic bone in your body, this book will have you producing boutique-worthy vegan food gifts. To get things started, we'll begin with an entire chapter devoted to getting your packaging skills up to snuff. Included will be templates, patterns, and directions for cutting, folding, and making your own gift bags, boxes, and other packages. There are even gift tags and recipe cards designed and illustrated by Kurt Halsey for you to copy and use on all of your delicious presents.

Next up are the recipes, which cover everything from ready-to-gift sweet and savory treats, to ready-to-make mixes, to preserves, sauces, cookies, seasonings, and even homemade liqueurs! Each recipe will also include packaging ideas. I've done my best to include recipes that aren't too foreign and to use ingredients that you can easily find at your local market.

Recipe and Project Icon Key

Level of Difficulty:	★ = easy
	★ ★ = medium difficulty
	★ ★ ★ = a bit more time required, but you can do it!
Cost:	$ = under $5 (£3) per gift
	$$ = more than $5 (£3), but less than $20 (£13) per gift
	$$$ = more than $20 (£13) per gift
Speed/Quantity:	⚡ = great projects to do quickly and/or en masse (think bake sales and holiday gift giving.)

Now let's talk a little bit about containers. There are so many choices when it comes to packaging your food gifts. How do you choose? I have spent many a dollar on gift bags, boxes, and tins in years passed. But now I say, "Phooey!" to those disposable decorative displays and make my own whenever possible. Of course, I can't make my own packaging for everything and in those cases I hit up thrift stores, garage sales, and flea markets—all great resources for old and beautiful bottles, tins, and jars full of character. Discount stores and dollar stores are also indispensable when it comes to cheap containers. I am constantly clearing the shelves at my local store of all of their seasoning shaker jars—they are only a dollar! As long as you give all of these items a good washing, they are great for gifting.

Along those same lines, recycle! (Or rather, I should say, "up-cycle!") Give empty containers new life. I almost never throw out glass bottles and jars, because I know I can refill them with something delicious. I soak them in warm sudsy water, remove the old labels, and add my own custom tags. Keep a particular eye out for unique bottles from microbreweries and small distilleries; they often carry amazing bottles with their own self-sealing (swing-top) caps.

Finally, check online. When all else fails, anything can be bought online these days. From Etsy to Amazon, the Web is your oyster, especially if you have your heart set on a certain look. In the Resources section, at the end of the book, you will find a list of suppliers and products that I use and recommend for the projects in this book.

Now let's have some fun! Grab your scissors and your measuring spoons—we are about to get crafty, folks! And your friends and family (and even those unsuspecting meat eaters!) will get to reap all the delicious rewards—just don't forget to save some for yourself!

Chapter 1

Cut Along the Dotted Line

Easy Peasy Packaging Ideas and Basics

Here you will find instructions and templates for basic folding techniques from a super simple no-glue gift bag to handmade cupcake and muffin liners, loaf pans, boxes, recipe books, and more. There will also be illustrated gift tags, potluck tent cards, and recipe cards that can be copied and used on all your delicious presents.

Super Simple Gift Envelope

I wasn't going to include this in the book, because it seems so, I dunno, like, duh, but so many people have commented on them when I give gifts packed up in them that I figured I would include them as an option.

Paper

Tape or glue

Hole punch

Ribbon, yarn, or twine

1. Place the sheet of paper facedown on a flat surface.
2. Fold the right edge of the paper toward the center.
3. Fold the left edge of the paper toward the center so that it overlaps the right edge by about ½ inch (1.3 cm), and tape or glue in place.
4. Fold both bottom corners up and inward.
5. Fold the bottom edge up and tape or glue in place.
6. Fill with treats.
7. Fold the top edge over and punch two holes about 1 inch (2.5 cm) apart.
8. Flip over, thread the ribbon through the holes, and tie closed.

Double Pocket Gift Bag

This bag is great to use when you want to keep two kinds of treats separated! Not only is it super easy to make, but it can also be made in pretty much any size. Better yet, it requires no adhesive! You can make it out of waxed paper, parchment paper, or in a pinch, you could even use newspaper! For ease of instruction, I will give you specific measurements here, and then you can play around with the process to make it any size you want. I make little ones out of regular letter-size sheets of paper, and staple the tops closed. This makes the perfect size for two cookies, to give as gifts to large groups. Also, it's a fun way to package cookies for bake sales (use clear cellophane); include a business card or a price tag with the ingredients listed.

Ruler

Scissors

Paper

Hole punch

Ribbon or twine

Gift tag or label

1. Cut a piece of paper 24-inches (60 cm) long by 12 inches (30 cm)-wide.
2. Bring the long ends together.
3. Fold the long ends together into 1-inch (2.5 cm) folds, twice, to make a seam.
4. After you fold it twice, open it up so it looks like a paper towel roll, using your thumb and forefinger to hold the fold and your other fingers to open it up. Now lay it down and put the fold in the middle like a seam and flatten, creasing the two outer edges.
5. Fold in half by bringing the two open short ends together.
6. Fill each side with treats.
7. Fold the top down twice in 1-inch (2.5 cm) folds to seal.
8. Punch two holes about 2 inches (5 cm) apart in the folded top, thread with ribbon or twine, and tie closed.
9. Affix a Hang Tag (pages 30–33) or Label (pages 30–31).

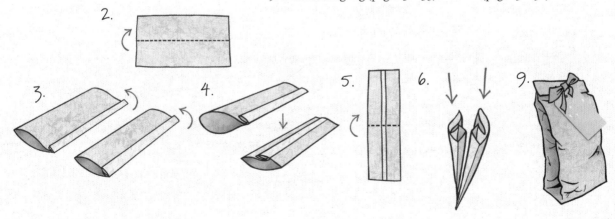

Truffle Gift Box

This little box is super-duper easy to make and super cute, too! You can use any kind of craft paper. I like the thicker scrapbook papers because they are often double sided, already measure 12 x 12 inches (30 x 30 cm), and come in so many awesome patterns. Just think of the ways you can customize these with different holiday papers! This one does require an adhesive, and I like to use a glue stick because it dries so quickly (according to the company's website, Elmer's glue contains no animal products), but you can use tape or even a stapler if you choose.

Ruler

12 x 12-inch (30 x 30 cm) piece of craft paper

Scissors

Glue

1. Measure 1½ inches (3.8 cm) from the bottom of the paper and fold up. Crease. Repeat at the top of the paper.
2. Bring the crease of the bottom folded edge up to meet the open end of the top folded edge. Fold to create a crease just shy of the center of the page. Unfold. Repeat with the top of the paper. This will create a 1½-inch (3.8 cm) space between the creases in the center of the paper. Unfold everything so the paper is flat.
3. Now fold in the right edge 1½ inches (3.8 cm) and crease. Repeat with the left edge. Unfold both edges.
4. Using scissors, cut each of the tabs along the folded lines up to the crease. There will be eight cuts total.
5. Fold in the small tabs and apply a bit of glue to each tab.
6. Glue each tab to the inside of the flaps; four to form the box, and two to form the lid.

Gift It!

Use these boxes to package Cake Truffles (page 60), Choconut Mounds (page 59), or Peanut Butter Balls (page 63).

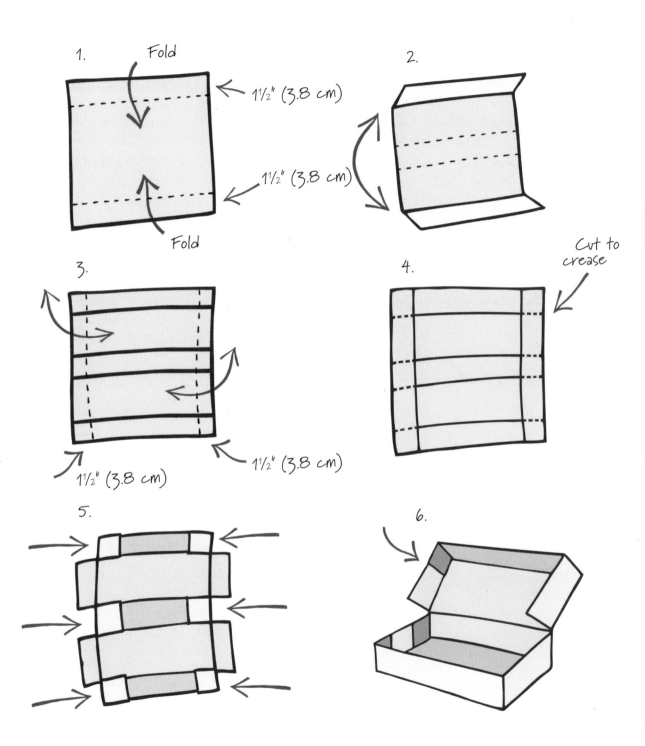

1. Fold

1½" (3.8 cm)

1½" (3.8 cm)

Fold

2.

3.

1½" (3.8 cm)

1½" (3.8 cm)

4.

Cut to crease

5.

6.

Window Treat Box

This box is the perfect size for gifting a single cupcake or a stack of cookies. (I promise I won't tell if you use it to package up nonfood gifts as well!) You can make this box with or without the window. It's cute either way.

2 sheets of craft paper, 12 x 12 inches (30 x 30 cm)

Ruler

Scissors or craft knife

Piece of cellophane, 4 x 4 inches (10 x 10 cm)

Glue or double-sided tape

You will follow the same process for the lid and the bottom. The only exception is the window. There is no need to cut a window in the bottom.

1. To make the lid, fold one sheet into a grid of nine squares. Each square on the grid will measure 4 x 4 inches (10 x 10 cm). Then unfold and lay flat.
2. Measure a square inside the center square, leaving a ½-inch (1.3 cm) border. This will be the window.
3. Using scissors or a craft knife, cut an X in the center window.
4. Fold each triangle back to create a square opening.
5. Trim the excess, leaving the ½-inch (1.3 cm) border. (The purpose of this step is to have a clean edge versus a raw edge on the outside of the box.)
6. Attach the cellophane with glue (or double-sided tape) and allow to dry.
7. Fold each corner on the diagonal. These folds will create flaps that will fold inside the box.
8. Attach the flaps to the inside panels of the box with glue, double-sided tape, or even a single staple.
9. Repeat the process with the second sheet of paper for the bottom of the box, omitting the window in steps 2 through 6. To make sure your lid fits easily onto your box, trim your 12 x 12-inch (30 x 30 cm) sheet to 11½ x 11½ inches (29 x 29 cm). Fold into a grid of nine squares, with each square measuring about 3⅚ inches (9.6 cm) square. Don't put too much emphasis on exact measurements; just make sure the center square is a tad bit smaller than the lid's center square, and your lid should fit properly on the box.
10. Fill with treats and place the lid on the box.

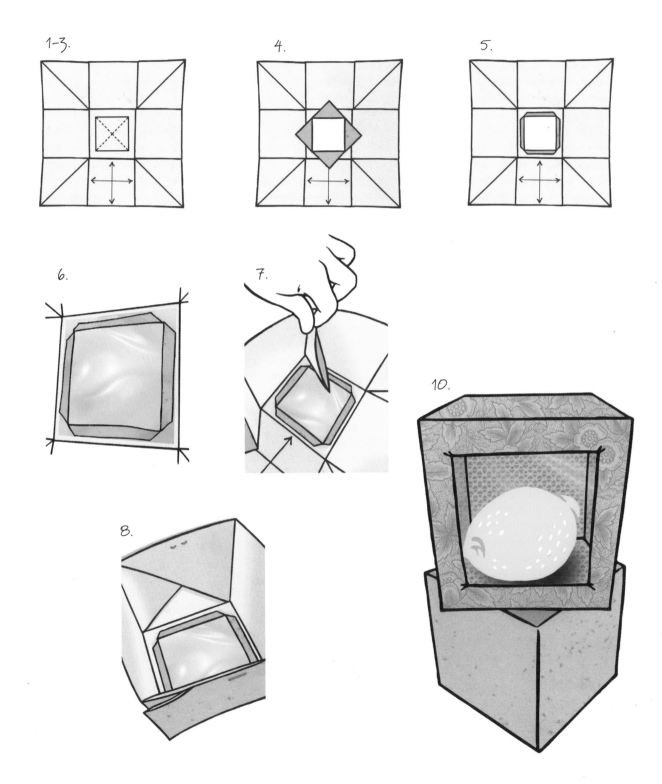

1-3.

4.

5.

6.

7.

8.

10.

Reusable Felt Gift Bag

Perusing the aisles of my local craft store I came across these 9 x 12-inch (23 x 30 cm) felt sheets, made from 100 percent post-consumer recycled plastic bottles, for only 20 cents apiece. That's five for a dollar, folks! And because these bags can be made in any size, and most sizes require only two sheets, well, that's less than 50 cents a bag! Oh, and I can whip one up in about 20 minutes, so once you get the hang of it, you will be able to make a bazillion of these in time for the holidays. They are perfect to fill with cellophane bags of treats. Or, maybe tuck a Truffle Gift Box (page 14) in one. Or maybe fill one up with Twigs and Berries (page 72), because that's all vegans eat anyhow, right? You can cut all kinds of patterns and do all sorts of decorating with these bags. You can embroider the fronts, use hole punches to create patterns, appliqué felt shapes … the possibilities are truly endless. Have fun!

Ruler

Scissors

2 felt sheets

Metal yarn needle (or large-eye needle)

Yarn

(For ease of instruction, I will give you measurements here, but once you understand the concept, you can make them any size you want.)

1. Measure and cut your felt. You will need two 6 x 9-inch (15 x 23 cm) rectangles for the sides and one piece cut into the shape of a football, measuring 6 ½ inches (16 cm) from end to end and 5 inches (12.5 cm) across at its widest point for the bottom.
2. If you want to have built-in handles, cut the long end of each rectangle into a curve, and cut out the handle holes. (See the dotted lines on the pattern at right.) Otherwise, cut two additional felt strips to the desired handle length. You can attach these later.
3. Thread your yarn needle with a long length of yarn and sew one side of the bag to the bottom of the bag using a simple overcast stitch (see diagram at right).
4. Once you have attached both sides to the bottom, using the same overcast stitch, sew up the sides to complete the bag.
5. If attaching handles, do so using a simple X stitch.

1.

2.

3.

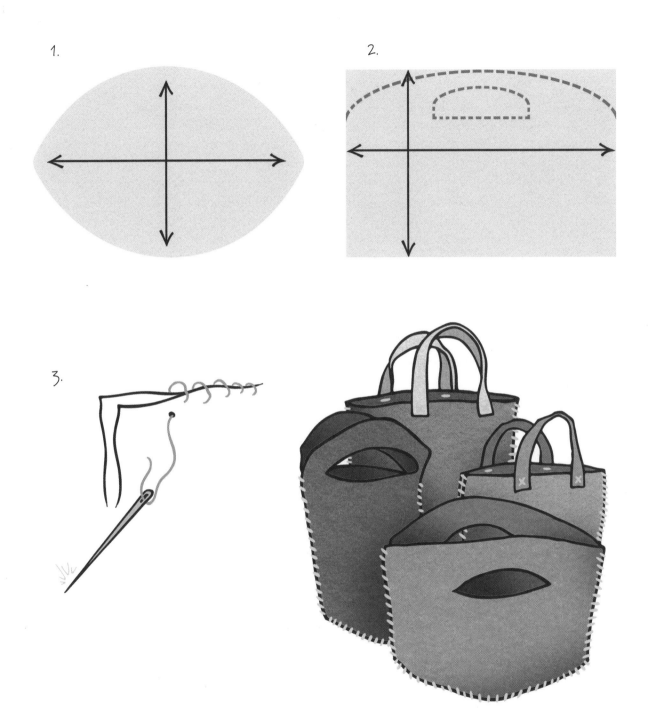

Fold-Your-Own Loaf Pan

For this project, I suggest using baking paper, parchment, or butcher paper. Remember that paper burns at 425°F (218°C), so don't ever use a homemade loaf pan for high-temperature baking. You can also make these out of decorative paper to place over the parchment ones for gifting.

12 x 12-inch (30 x 30 cm) sheet of paper

1. Start by folding the paper in half, then unfold.
2. Fold the outer edges in to meet the center crease.
3. Fold the inner edges back out to the outside, then flip over the paper.
4. Fold the outer edges up to the center line, crease, and then unfold and press flat.
5. Bring the bottom corner up to the third crease, then flatten.
6. Tuck the corner under.
7. Fold up other corner to make a point. Tuck it into the first corner.
8. Fold the point up and tuck in.
9. Repeat at other end.
10. Pull the sides out to form the pan.

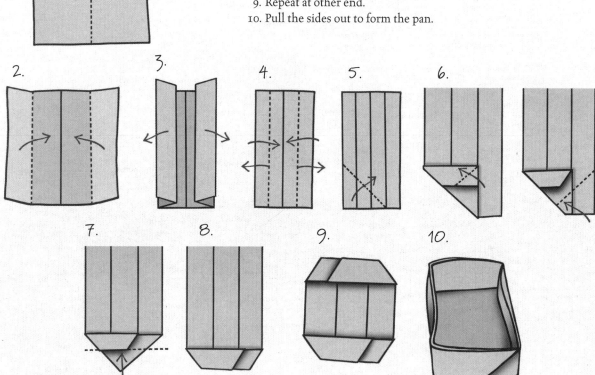

Parchment Baking Cups

Okay, I know that you can buy a package of, like, 10,000 paper baking cups for a dollar, but these are so cute, are really, really easy to make, and make a very special display for your cupcakes and muffins. You will only bake in the parchment paper, so you can choose any type of paper you like for the outside decorative layer. Use wrapping paper, origami paper, craft paper, or just the parchment for a simple, elegant look. Imagine making custom papers for wedding showers, baby showers, and birthday parties.

Pint glass (or other tapered glass that has a bottom that fits inside a standard muffin tin)

12 squares of parchment paper, 6 x 6 inches (15 x 15 cm)

12 squares of decorative paper, 6 x 6 inches (15 x 15 cm)

Ribbon or twine

1. Place the pint glass upside down on a flat surface.
2. Center a square of parchment on the bottom of the glass.
3. Using both hands, firmly press the paper around the glass to form a cup.
4. Repeat a few times to make sure the paper is folded and creased well and will hold its shape.
5. Remove the paper from the glass, and repeat with the remaining parchment. Use the parchment cups for baking.
6. Repeat the process with the decorative papers.
7. Place the baked goods in the parchment cups inside the decorative cups for a layered look.
8. Tie ribbon or twine around the cups for a festive look.

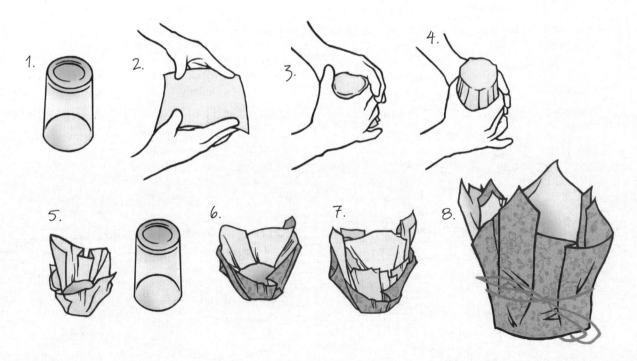

Simple Paper Flower

This paper flower can be just that—simple. Or, you can take it to a million different levels. You can curl the edges of your papers, paint them, add glitter, use more layers, or make two and glue them back to back.

Pencil

Cardstock

Scissors

Glue

Stapler (optional)

Buttons or other small notions

Popsicle stick (optional)

1. With pencil, trace the flower pattern (or draw your own) four times onto cardstock.
2. Cut out the flower shapes.
3. Layer one on top of the other, as shown in the diagram.
4. Repeat until all four flowers are used.
5. Glue or staple in place.
6. Fold the petals upward to create a three-dimensional effect.
7. Glue a button or other notion (fuzzy pom-poms are fun!) in the center of the flower.
8. Add a Popsicle stick as a stem, if desired.

Gift It!

These look great in the center of a "Pot" Brownie (page 49) or as a decorative top for the Recipe Treasure Box (page 26). They also work well pressed into muffins or cupcakes or glued on the top of a mason jar.

1.

2.

3.

4.

5.

6.

7.

8.

Double-Sided Cookbook

This gift is not a gift of food, but it is a food gift! It makes a wonderful gift for a foodie friend or family member. Imagine how special a book filled with treasured family recipes would be! Or give it as a guide for a new vegan, filled with your personal tips and favorite vegan recipes. Go crazy! Here is where you can let your creative juices flow. Make it simple, or make it garish, or make it elegant, or make it cute. The options are really limitless. Make it any way you want, just make sure that you make it personal, and make it with love. And remember, it doesn't have to be perfect— it's handmade! Once you realize how this works, you can make them in any size. For ease of instruction, I give specific measurements.

2 pieces of decorative paper for the covers, 6 x 6 inches (15 x 15 cm)

2 pieces of chipboard, 4 ½ x 4 ½ inches (11.5 x 11.5 cm)

Glue

1 strip of plain paper, 4 x 64 inches (10 x 160 cm)*

Scissors

Pens, paint, pencils, magazine clippings, and so on, for decorating

* You can make short pieces of paper into one long strip by overlapping them and gluing them together. I use three strips cut from a sheet of 18 x 24-inch (45 x 60 cm) drawing paper. Just make sure the length of the final strip is divisible by 4 inches (10 cm).

1. First, make the covers. Place the decorative paper facedown on a flat surface. Center the chipboard on the decorative paper and glue in place.
2. Fold the corners over the chipboard and glue in place.
3. Fold the edges over and glue in place.
4. Repeat with the other cover and set aside to dry.
5. Make the inside pages. Fold the long strip of paper like an accordion into 4-inch (10 cm) pages. (You can make your book with more or less pages by adjusting the length of the strip, keeping it divisible by 4 inches [10 cm].)
6. Glue the first page to the inside of the cover and glue the last page to the inside of the other cover. Allow to dry.
7. Decorate the covers with pens, paint, or whatever you fancy.
8. Decorate and fill the pages!

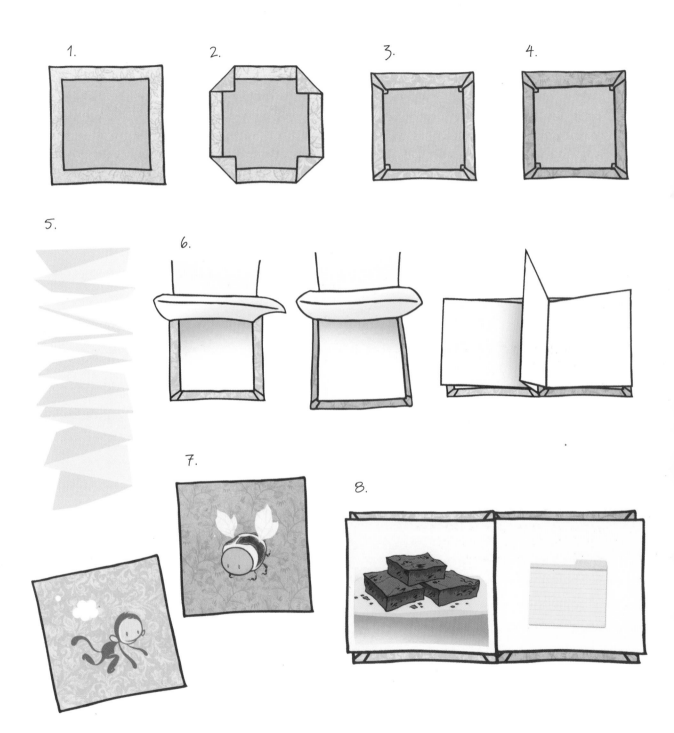

1.

2.

3.

4.

5.

6.

7.

8.

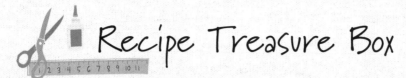

Recipe Treasure Box

This handmade recipe box is meant to be given as a gift full of your beloved recipes and family favorites—true treasures! You can make it with plain white paper, for a blank canvas for decorating; however, if you start out with a pretty printed paper, it will already be decorated! Add beads for feet, glue Simple Paper Flowers (page 22) to the top, decoupage images cut from magazines or photos, line the inside with felt or fabric . . . have fun with it. There are some awesome blank recipe cards on pages 28–29 for you to copy onto cardstock and place inside your beautiful treasure box.

Sheet of 18 x 24-inch (45 x 60 cm) paper

Chipboard cut into the following shapes:

A. 1 rectangle, 4¼ x 5¼ inches (10.5 x 13 cm)

B. 3 rectangles, 4 x 5 inches (10 x 12.5 cm)

C. 2 squares, 4 x 4 inches (10 x 10 cm)

D. 2 rectangles, 4¼ x 1 inch (10.5 x 2.5 cm)

E. 1 rectangle, 5¼ x 1 inch (13 x 2.5 cm)

Glue

Ruler

Pencil

Scissors

Paint, pens, markers, decoupage materials, etc., for decorating

1. Place the sheet of paper face down on a flat surface and arrange the chipboard as shown in the diagram. The largest rectangle will be at the far left, and it will become the lid. Glue in place, being sure to leave about ⅛ inch (6 mm) of space between all of the pieces. From here on out, the left side will be referred to as the lid and the right side will be referred to as the box.

2. Trace the outside of the entire shape in pencil, leaving a 1-inch (2.5 cm) border all around. Cut out.

3. Cut diagonal slits at the corners as shown by the black lines on the diagram.

4. Fold over the corners and flaps on the box and lid as shown in the diagram and glue in place.

5. Fold over the flaps on the lid and glue in place, leaving the two tabs on the box and the two tabs in the center unfolded. You will use these tabs later, to form the box.

6. Fold over the flaps on the lid and glue in place.

7. Form the lid by attaching the short tabs to the inside of the chipboard and gluing in place. Then fold over the long tab to create a finished edge. Glue in place.

8. Form the front of the box by folding up the front panel and gluing the tabs to the outside of the side panel. Repeat on the other side.

9. Finish the box by folding up the center panel (the back of the box) and gluing the tabs to the outside of the box.

10. Decorate!

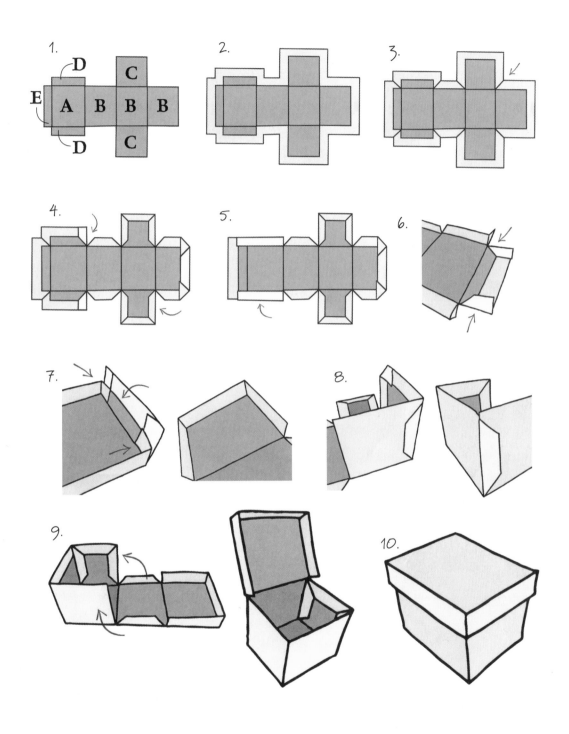

1.

D
E
A B B B
D
C
C

On the next few pages, you will find beautifully designed and illustrated hang tags, labels, recipe cards, and even potluck table tents! Please take these templates and scan or copy them, print them, and cut them out to use on all of your homemade projects.

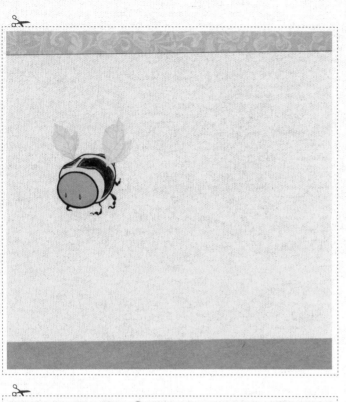

LOTNICZA
PAR AVION

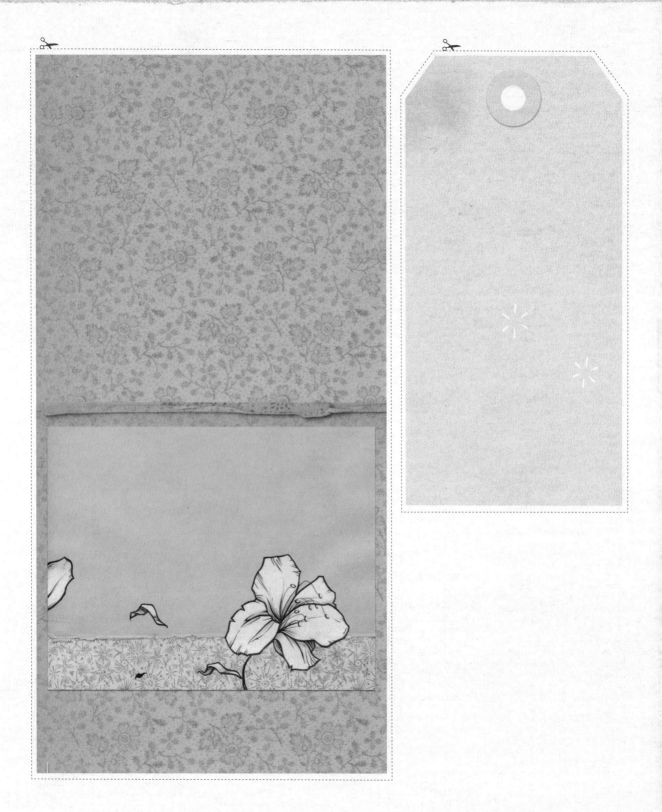

Chapter 2

Ready to Gift

Delicious Gifts Ready for Immediate Enjoyment

This chapter is where you will find all the recipes needed to put together delicious, ready-to-eat treats, from chocolate chip cookies, to lemon poppy seed cakes, to peanut butter truffles packed in pretty homemade boxes. Almost every recipe comes with a suggestion for packaging, so you can go forth and create delectable endowments that will wow the gifted not only with their delicious flavors, but also with that undoubtedly delightful handmade touch.

Cool
Lemon
Cookies

Cool Lemon Cookies

These are reminiscent of the lemon coolers of years passed.
Sweet and tart and cool, these delicious little cookies are so yummy,
you won't mind the sugary mess on your fingers!

For Cookies:

½ cup (60 g) powdered sugar

½ cup (100 g) granulated sugar

⅓ cup (64 g) vegetable shortening

6 ounces (170 g) nondairy yogurt

1 teaspoon vanilla extract

1 teaspoon lemon extract

¼ teaspoon salt

2 ½ cups (313 g) all-purpose flour

1 ½ teaspoons baking powder

1 teaspoon baking soda

For Coating:

1 cup (120 g) powdered sugar

1 envelope (¼ ounce, or 7 g)
  unsweetened lemonade drink mix
  powder, such as Kool-Aid

Preheat the oven to 325°F (170°C, or gas mark 3).

Have ready 2 baking sheets lined with parchment or silicone baking mats such as Silpat.

To make the cookies: Combine the powdered sugar, granulated sugar, shortening, yogurt, vanilla and lemon extracts, and salt in a large mixing bowl and beat with an electric mixer until creamy.

In a separate bowl, sift together the flour, baking powder, and baking soda. Slowly add to the sugar mixture and beat until smooth.

Spoon drop about 1 ounce (28 g) per cookie onto the prepared baking sheets. Place 15 cookies evenly spaced on each baking sheet.

Bake for 18 to 20 minutes, or until lightly browned.

While the cookies are baking, make the coating: Place the powdered sugar and drink mix in a resealable plastic bag and shake to combine.

Remove the cookies from the oven and allow to cool on the pan for about 5 minutes.

Add the cookies, about 4 or 5 at a time, to the bag and shake to coat.

YIELD: 30 cookies

Gift It!

As with all cookies, these look great packaged in all kinds of ways: bags, baskets, boxes, or trays. However you decide to pack them up, make sure to add a pretty Hang Tag (pages 30–33).

Peanut Butter Chocolate Chip Cookies

A classic combo of peanut butter and chocolate in cookie form

2 cups (512 g) creamy peanut butter

1 cup (235 ml) nondairy milk

½ cup (100 g) granulated sugar

½ cup (110 g) firmly packed brown sugar

¼ cup (60 ml) canola or other mild-flavored vegetable oil

¼ cup (60 ml) maple syrup

2 teaspoons vanilla extract

3 cups (375 g) all-purpose flour

½ teaspoon baking soda

½ teaspoon baking powder

½ teaspoon salt

1 cup (176 g) vegan chocolate chips

Preheat the oven to 350°F (180°C, or gas mark 4).

Line 4 baking sheets with parchment or silicone baking mats, such as Silpat.

Combine the peanut butter, milk, granulated sugar, brown sugar, oil, maple syrup, and vanilla in a large mixing bowl. Using an electric beater, beat until smooth.

In a separate bowl, sift together the flour, baking soda, baking powder, and salt. Add to the sugar mixture and beat until you get a smooth, shiny dough. Depending on the moisture content of your peanut butter, you may need to add a little more or little less flour.

Fold in the chocolate chips.

Roll about 2 tablespoons (40 g) of dough per cookie into a ball and place on the prepared baking sheets. Place 12 cookies evenly spaced on each baking sheet. Flatten slightly with the tines of a fork to create the trademark hashmarks almost always found atop peanut butter cookies.

Bake for 15 to 18 minutes, until slightly browned on the bottoms and edges.

Remove from the oven. Allow to cool for 5 minutes before transferring to a cooling rack to cool completely.

YIELD: 48 cookies

Gift It!

As with all cookies, these look great packaged in all kinds of ways: bags, baskets, boxes, or trays. However you decide to pack them up, be sure to add a pretty Hang Tag (pages 30–33) and note that they contain peanuts.

Cranberry-Walnut Oatmeal Cookies

I just keep telling myself that because they are made from oatmeal, it's okay to have cookies for breakfast.

2 cups (156 g) quick-cooking oats

2 cups (250 g) all-purpose flour

1 teaspoon baking soda

½ teaspoon salt

¼ teaspoon nutmeg

1 cup (220 g) firmly packed brown sugar

1 cup (235 ml) almond, coconut, or soy milk

½ cup (120 ml) canola or other mild-flavored vegetable oil

¼ cup (60 ml) maple syrup

1 teaspoon vanilla extract

1 cup (120 g) chopped walnuts (optional for those with nut allergies)

1 cup (122 g) dried cranberries

Preheat the oven to 350°F (180°C, or gas mark 4).

Line 3 baking sheets with parchment or silicone baking mats.

In a large bowl, mix together the oats, flour, baking soda, salt, and nutmeg.

In a separate bowl, mix together the brown sugar, milk, oil, syrup, and vanilla until smooth.

Add the wet ingredients to the dry and mix until well combined and goopy.

Fold in the walnuts and cranberries.

Drop a heaping 2 tablespoons (about 50 g) of dough onto the prepared baking sheets, spacing them about 2 inches (5 cm) apart and placing 12 cookies per sheet.

Bake for 15 to 18 minutes, or until golden brown around the edges.

Allow to cool for 5 minutes before transferring to a cooling rack to cool completely.

YIELD: 36 cookies

Gift It!

Place in a cellophane bag, in a gift basket, or on a platter. They package up nicely alongside some Instant Hot Cocoa Mix (page 112) and/or a few teabags tucked into a mug.

Amazingly Ambitious Sugar Cookies

Seriously, is there anything a good sugar cookie can't do?
This recipe is for basic sugar cookie dough, plus a couple of fun things to do with it.

For Cookies:

1 cup (224 g) nondairy butter

1 cup (200 g) evaporated cane juice

¼ cup (60 g) nondairy yogurt (vanilla or plain)

1 tablespoon (15 ml) vanilla extract

3 cups (375 g) all-purpose flour

1 teaspoon baking powder

½ teaspoon baking soda

½ teaspoon sea salt

For Icing (optional):

3 cups (360 g) powdered sugar

3 tablespoons (45 ml) soy milk

1 teaspoon vanilla extract

Food coloring (optional)

Chocolate chips (optional)

Candy canes (optional)

To make the cookies: With an electric mixer, cream together the butter and cane juice until fluffy.

Add the yogurt and vanilla extract and beat to combine.

In a separate bowl, sift together the flour, baking powder, baking soda, and salt. Add to the sugar mixture and beat until well combined.

Divide into 4 equal pieces, wrap in plastic wrap or waxed paper, and refrigerate at least 1 hour. Use as desired (see below).

To make the icing: Whisk or beat together the sugar, milk, and vanilla until smooth. Add the food coloring as desired. Apply to completely cool cookies, and let dry on a cooling rack to harden completely before packaging.

Chocolate Dippers

Preheat the oven to 350°F (180°C, or gas mark 4). Have ready 3 baking sheets lined with parchment or silicone baking mats.

Roll out one piece of dough at a time to ⅛ inch (3 mm) thick on a well-floured surface. Use a 3-inch (7.5 cm) round cookie cutter (or a pint glass) to cut out round cookies. Gather up the scraps of dough and repeat the process. Repeat with the remaining dough.

Place the cookies on the prepared baking sheets, 12 cookies per sheet.

Bake for about 10 minutes, or until slightly browned.

Let cool for 5 minutes before transferring to a wire rack to cool completely.

In a double boiler, melt 12 ounces (340 g) vegan chocolate chips. Dip one half of the cookie into the chocolate and then set on waxed paper to cool and harden.

You can sprinkle on broken candy canes for extra holiday goodness.

Holiday Cutouts

Preheat the oven to 350°F (180°C, or gas mark 4). Have ready
3 baking sheets lined with parchment or silicone baking mats.

Roll out one piece of dough at a time on a well-floured surface and cut into desired shapes with cookie cutters. Gather up the scraps of dough and repeat the process. Repeat with the remaining dough.

Place the cutouts on the prepared baking sheets, 12 cookies per sheet.

Bake for 10 to 12 minutes, or until just slightly browned around the edges.

Allow to cool for 5 minutes before transferring to a cooling rack to cool completely before icing.

YIELD: About 3 dozen cookies, depending on the size of your cookie cutters

Gift It!

Cookies look great in all kinds of packaging! These ones look particularly fabulous where they can be showcased, as in the Window Treat Box (page 16), or simply placed in clear cellophane bags. Either way, tie on a Hang Tag (pages 30–33) with a nice pretty ribbon.

Orange Chocolate Linzers

Specialty linzer cookie cutters are widely available at baking supply shops and online. If you don't have one (or don't want one) you can simply use graduated round cookie cutters, 2 inches (5 cm) for the outer circle and 1 inch (2.5 cm) for the inner circle.

For Cookies:

1 ⅔ cups (280 g) all-purpose flour

¼ teaspoon baking powder

¼ teaspoon salt

¾ cup (150 g) evaporated cane juice or granulated sugar

½ cup (112 g) nondairy butter

¼ cup (60 ml) orange juice

1 teaspoon vanilla extract

1 teaspoon orange extract

Powdered sugar, for sprinkling

For Ganache Filling:

½ cup (120 ml) nondairy cream (full-fat coconut milk, MimicCreme, or soy or coconut creamer)

1 cup (176 g) vegan chocolate chips

1 tablespoon (15 ml) orange extract

To make the cookies: In a small mixing bowl, sift together the flour, baking powder, and salt.

In a large mixing bowl, beat together the evaporated cane juice, butter, orange juice, vanilla, and orange extract until well combined. The butter will separate; that is normal.

Slowly add in the flour mixture and beat until well combined.

Turn out the dough onto a floured surface and knead into a soft, smooth dough. Shape into a ball, wrap in plastic, and refrigerate for at least 2 hours, or until ready to bake.

Preheat the oven to 375°F (190°C, or gas mark 5). Line several baking sheets with parchment or silicone baking mats.

Remove the dough from the refrigerator. Divide the dough in half, so it is easier to work with. Roll out the dough on a well-floured surface until it is about ⅛ inch (3 mm) thick. Use a linzer cookie cutter (see headnote) to cut 36 tops and 36 bottoms, gathering up the scraps and rerolling as needed. Transfer to the prepared baking sheets.

Bake for 8 to 10 minutes, or until golden and the bottom and edges are lightly browned. Remove from the oven and transfer to a cooling rack to cool completely.

Sprinkle the powdered sugar all over the tops.

Meanwhile, make the filling: In a small saucepot, heat the cream until it just begins to boil. Remove from the heat and stir in the chocolate chips and orange extract until completely melted, combined, and smooth.

When the cookies are cool, spread about 1 teaspoon of ganache onto a cookie bottom and place a cookie top on top. Return to the rack and allow the ganache to cool and stiffen completely before packaging.

YIELD: 36 sandwich cookies

Gift It!

Because these ones are so pretty, I suggest packing them in a way that shows them off, in a clear cellophane bag with a pretty bow and Hang Tag (pages 30–33).

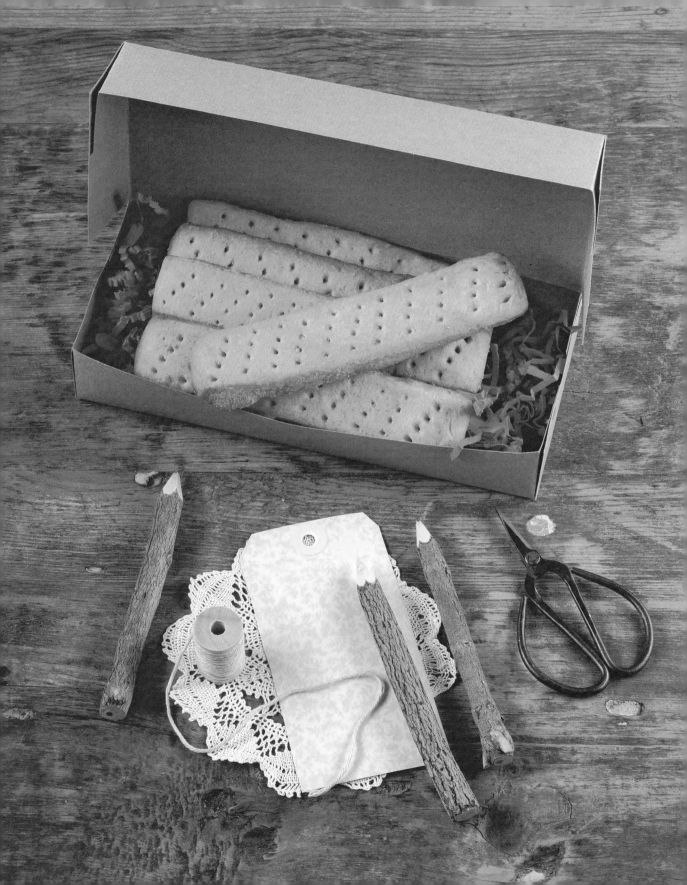

Shortbread Fingers

Because the main flavor in these not-very-sweet cookies comes from nondairy butter, choose wisely. Some nondairy butters are not as yummy as others. I really like Earth Balance Coconut Spread in these, but regular Earth Balance and Nucoa both work well, too.

½ cup (110 g) firmly packed brown sugar

1 cup (224 g) nondairy butter

¼ teaspoon salt

2 ¼ cups (281 g) all-purpose flour, divided

Preheat the oven to 325°F (170°C, or gas mark 3). Line a baking sheet with parchment or a silicone baking mat.

Using an electric mixer, cream together the brown sugar and butter. Add the salt and mix to combine. Add 2 cups (250 g) of the flour and mix well. The mixture will be crumbly.

Turn the mixture out onto a floured work surface and knead for about 5 minutes, adding the remaining ¼ cup (31 g) flour as needed to make a soft dough.

Roll out into a rectangle 5 x 12 inches (12.5 x 30 cm). Cut into twelve 1 x 5-inch (2.5 x 12.5 cm) fingers.

Prick the tops with the tines of a fork and arrange the fingers on the baking sheet, spacing them 1 inch (2.5 cm) apart.

Bake for 20 to 25 minutes, or until golden.

Allow to cool completely before removing from the baking sheet.

YIELD: 12 fingers

Note: This dough makes for a pretty good piecrust, too!

Gift It!

These make a fabulous accompaniment when gifting a jar of homemade Lemon Lavender Curd (page 145), Orange Basil Marmalade (page 143), or Classic Strawberry Jam (page 141).

S'more Brownies

I know that these are called S'more Brownies. I also know that s'mores call for graham crackers. I also know that most graham crackers have honey in them. Unless you are going to bake your own graham crackers, or have a good source for vegan ones, just use animal crackers. No one will be the wiser.

¼ cup (26 g) flaxseed meal

½ cup (120 ml) warm water

2 cups (250 g) all-purpose flour

1 cup (80 g) cocoa powder

½ teaspoon baking soda

½ teaspoon baking powder

¼ teaspoon salt

1 cup (200 g) sugar

½ cup (120 ml) canola oil or other mild-flavored vegetable oil

1 banana, mashed

1 cup (235 ml) nondairy milk

1 teaspoon vanilla extract

2 cups (352 g) vegan chocolate chips

1 (10-ounce, or 283 g) package vegan marshmallows, such as Dandies or Sweet & Sara, divided

1 cup (120 g) crushed vegan graham crackers or animal crackers, divided

Preheat the oven to 350°F (180°C, or gas mark 4). Coat a 9 x 13-inch (23 x 33 cm) baking dish with nonstick cooking spray.

In a small bowl, whisk together the flaxseed meal and warm water and set aside.

In a large mixing bowl, sift together the flour, cocoa, baking soda, baking powder, and salt.

In a separate mixing bowl, whisk together the sugar, oil, banana, milk, and vanilla until smooth. Add to the flour mixture and mix until well combined. Fold in the chocolate chips and half (5 ounces [142 g]) of the marshmallows. Spread evenly into the baking dish. Smooth the top with the back of a spoon. One by one, press the remaining marshmallows into the batter evenly across the top. Sprinkle the crushed graham crackers evenly over the top.

Bake for 30 to 40 minutes, or until firm and the marshmallows are golden and browned.

It's hard to check for doneness with the toothpick method, and all of the gooey goodness on top kind of makes it difficult to do the "dent" test, so you kinda have to jiggle the dish gently. It should be firm, not jiggly like pudding.

Allow to cool completely before attempting to cut these, or you will have a big mess. I know all the melty, gooey marshmallows are tempting, but wait or you will never get them cut properly.

Once completely cool, cut into squares.

YIELD: 15 brownies

Gift It!

You can package three in a Truffle Gift Box (page 14) or wrap individually in plastic wrap for bake sales or mini gifts (great for coworkers and classrooms!).

"Pot" Brownies

Sure, it's a silly play on words, but it is a really cute way to make brownies!

1 recipe Fudgy Brownie Mix (page 84)

Preheat oven to 350°F (180°C, or gas mark 4). Prepare 8 unglazed 3-inch (7.5 cm) terra-cotta pots for baking. Remove any labels, rinse the pots in clean water, and allow to dry. Do not wash with soap, because terra cotta is very porous and will absorb the detergent. Cut parchment or foil circles to fit into the bottom of the pot to cover the drainage hole.* Brush the entire inside surface of the pots liberally with vegetable oil or melted shortening.

Fill the pots just under three-fourths full with the brownie mix. Do not overfill or the brownies will spill over.

Place the pots on a baking sheet and bake for 55 to 60 minutes, or until a toothpick inserted into the center comes out clean.

Allow to cool completely before packaging for gifts.

YIELD: 8 pot brownies

* If you feel uncomfortable baking directly in a flowerpot (I've done lots of Internet research on this, so please make your own decisions!), you can line the inside of the flowerpots with aluminum foil or parchment. If using parchment, you can use the same method as the Parchment Baking Cups (page 21), turning the pot upside down to use as a mold. I admit that lining them with parchment makes eating them much easier, and makes cleanup a snap.

Gift It!

You can wrap these in clear cellophane, tying the top with a pretty ribbon. Another option is to place a Simple Paper Flower (page 22) glued onto a Popsicle stick in the center, like it is growing right out of the brownie!

G'Mornin' Muffins

Blueberry? Check. Lemon? Check. These fluffy muffins have all the makings of a delicious breakfast or an anytime snack. For a really special treat, how about adding homemade Classic Strawberry Jam (page 141)?

2 cups (250 g) all-purpose flour

3 tablespoons (24 g) arrowroot powder or cornstarch

1/2 teaspoon baking powder

1/2 teaspoon baking soda

1/2 teaspoon salt

1 cup (200 g) evaporated cane juice or granulated sugar

6 ounces (170 g) nondairy yogurt (lemon, vanilla, or plain)

1/2 cup (120 ml) canola or other mild-flavored vegetable oil

1/2 cup (120 ml) almond, coconut, or soy milk

1 teaspoon vanilla extract

1 teaspoon lemon extract

Zest and juice of 1 lemon

2 cups (290 g) blueberries, fresh or frozen (you may need to increase baking time if using frozen)

Preheat the oven to 350°F (180°C, or gas mark 4). Line a standard muffin tin with Parchment Baking Cups (page 21) as shown or use paper liners and 14 muffin cups.

In a large mixing bowl, sift together the flour, arrowroot, baking powder, baking soda, and salt.

In a separate bowl, mix together the evaporated cane juice, yogurt, oil, milk, vanilla, lemon, lemon zest, and lemon juice. Add to the flour mixture and mix until well combined, taking care not to overmix. Fold in the blueberries.

If using handmade liners, distribute the batter evenly among all 12 cups. If using standard papers, fill three-fourths full and you will get about 14 muffins.

Bake for 30 to 40 minutes (you will need less time for standard baking cups, more time for handmade cups), or until the tops are golden brown and a toothpick inserted into the center comes out clean.

Remove from the oven and allow to cool enough to touch, then transfer to a cooling rack to cool completely.

YIELD: 12 or 14 muffins

Gift It!

Pack up in a basket wrapped in cellophane or a pastry box tied up with a pretty ribbon.

Espresso Chocolate Chip Loaves

Before I started writing cookbooks, I was a real estate agent (I know, right?) and every year I would bake for all of my clients on all of the different holidays. I have probably gifted more than 200 of these cakes, not to mention the countless loaves I have made for vegan bake sales. They are a good, dependable gift. Who doesn't love chocolate cake?

6 ounces (170 g) plain or vanilla soy yogurt

1 cup (235 ml) canola oil

1 tablespoon (15 ml) vanilla extract

1 tablespoon (15 ml) chocolate extract, or more vanilla

2 cups (400 g) sugar

2 tablespoons (44 g) molasses

½ cup (120 ml) coffee-flavored liqueur, such as Kahlúa

1 cup (235 ml) vanilla or plain soy or other nondairy milk

½ cup (22 g) instant coffee crystals

3 ½ cups (438 g) all-purpose flour

1 cup (120 g) whole wheat pastry flour

½ cup (40 g) unsweetened cocoa powder

2 teaspoons baking powder

2 teaspoons baking soda

2 tablespoons (16 g) cornstarch

1 teaspoon salt

1 ½ cups (264 g) nondairy semisweet chocolate chips

To make the loaves: Preheat the oven to 350°F (180°C, or gas mark 4). Coat 5 mini loaf tins (5 x 3½ x 2 inches [12.5 x 8.3 x 5 cm]), or 2 standard loaf tins (9 x 5 x 3 inches [23 x 12.5 x 7.5 cm]) with nonstick cooking spray, or use Fold-Your-Own Loaf Pans (page 20).

In a large bowl, mix together the yogurt, oil, vanilla and chocolate extracts, sugar, molasses, coffee liqueur, milk, and coffee crystals.

In a separate bowl, sift together the flours, cocoa powder, baking powder, baking soda, cornstarch, and salt. Add to the sugar mixture and mix well. Fold in the chocolate chips.

Fill the loaf tins two-thirds full.

Bake for 35 to 45 minutes, or until a toothpick inserted into the center comes out clean. Let cool completely before turning out the loaves. If you are using mini loaf tins, bake for 45–60 minutes.

YIELD: 5 mini or 2 standard loaves

Gift It!

Wrap in plastic wrap or place in cellophane bags and attach a cute Label (pages 30–31) or tie on a pretty ribbon with a Hang Tag (pages 30–33).

Lemon Poppy Seed Cakes

Moist and delicious, these cakes have just enough sweetness and the right amount of tang. Be sure to keep at least one for yourself!

For Cakes:

2 (6-ounce, or 170 g each) containers lemon soy yogurt (plain or vanilla will work, too)

1 cup (235 ml) plain or vanilla soy or coconut milk

1 cup (235 ml) canola oil

2 cups (400 g) evaporated cane juice or granulated sugar

1 tablespoon (15 ml) vanilla extract

1 teaspoon lemon extract

Zest and juice of 1 lemon

½ cup (120 g) vegan sour cream

2 tablespoons (18 g) poppy seeds

5 cups (625 g) all-purpose flour

3 tablespoons (24 g) cornstarch

1 tablespoon (12 g) baking powder

1 tablespoon (12 g) baking soda

1 teaspoon salt

For Glaze (optional):

1 cup (120 g) powdered sugar

2 tablespoons (30 ml) lemon juice

To make the cakes: Preheat the oven to 350°F (180°C, or gas mark 4). Coat 5 mini loaf tins (5 x 3 ½ x 2 inches [12.5 x 8.3 x 5 cm]), or 2 standard loaf tins (9 x 5 x 3 inches [23 x 12.5 x 7.5 cm]) with nonstick cooking spray, or use Fold-Your-Own Loaf Pans (page 20).

In a large bowl, mix together the yogurt, milk, oil, evaporated cane juice, vanilla and lemon extracts, lemon zest and juice, sour cream, and poppy seeds.

In a separate bowl, sift together the flour, cornstarch, baking powder, baking soda, and salt. Add to the yogurt mixture and stir to combine. The mixture will be thick, not runny.

Fill the loaf tins two-thirds full.

Bake for about 45 minutes, or until a toothpick inserted into the center comes out clean. Let cool completely before turning out the loaves. If you are using mini loaf tins, bake for 45–60 minutes.

To make the glaze: Whisk together the powdered sugar and lemon juice until smooth, and then drizzle over the cakes.

YIELD: 5 mini or 2 standard loaves

Gift It!

Wrap in plastic wrap or place in cellophane bags and attach a cute Label (pages 30–31) or tie on a pretty ribbon with a Hang Tag (pages 30–33).

Pumpkin Chocolate Chip Loaf

Although these are yummy anytime of the year, I tend to
save this recipe for fall and winter holiday gifts.

3 cups (375 g) all-purpose flour

1 teaspoon baking soda

1 teaspoon baking powder

½ teaspoon salt

½ teaspoon ground cinnamon

½ teaspoon ground cloves

½ teaspoon ground nutmeg

3 ½ cups (15 ounces, or 425 g) pumpkin
    purée

1 cup (200 g) evaporated cane juice
    or sugar

½ cup (120 ml) soy, almond, or coconut
    milk

½ cup (120 ml) canola or other mild-
    flavored vegetable oil

1 teaspoon vanilla extract

1 cup (176 g) vegan chocolate chips

To make the loaves: Preheat the oven to 350°F (180°C, or
gas mark 4). Coat 5 mini loaf tins (5 x 3½ x 2 inches [12.5 x
8.3 x 5 cm]), or 2 standard loaf tins (9 x 5 x 3 inches [23 x 12.5
x 7.5 cm]) with nonstick cooking spray, or use Fold-Your-Own
Loaf Pans (page 20).

In a large mixing bowl, combine the flour, baking soda,
baking powder, salt, cinnamon, cloves, and nutmeg.

In a separate bowl, mix together the pumpkin, evaporated
cane juice, milk, oil, and vanilla. Add to the flour mixture and
stir to combine. Fold in the chocolate chips.

Fill each loaf tin three-fourths full and smooth the tops with
the back of a spoon.

Bake for 40 to 60 minutes, until the tops have cracked and a
toothpick inserted into the center comes out clean. If you are
using mini loaf tins, bake for 45–60 minutes.

Let cool completely before turning out the loaves.

YIELD: 5 mini or 2 standard loaves

Note: These freeze well!

Gift It!

Wrap in plastic wrap or place in cellophane
bags and attach a cute Label (pages 30–31)
or tie on a pretty ribbon with a Hang Tag
(pages 30–33).

Banana Nut Bread

This is a holiday classic, but if you ask me, there is no reason why we shouldn't enjoy this delicious bread ANY time of year. Fun fact: There are no "weird" vegan ingredients in these, so they are perfect for the skeptics in your life!

2 cups (250 g) all-purpose flour

1 teaspoon salt

½ teaspoon ground cinnamon

1 teaspoon baking soda

2 teaspoons baking powder

¼ cup (32 g) arrowroot powder or cornstarch

1 cup (200 g) evaporated cane juice or sugar

1 cup (120 g) chopped walnuts or pecans

½ cup (80 g) raisins (optional)

½ cup (120 ml) canola or other mild-flavored vegetable oil

1 ½ cups (338 g) mashed overripe banana

2 teaspoons (10 ml) vanilla extract

To make the loaves: Preheat the oven to 350°F (180°C, or gas mark 4). Coat 5 mini loaf tins (5 x 3½ x 2 inches [12.5 x 8.3 x 5 cm]), or 2 standard loaf tins (9 x 5 x 3 inches [23 x 12.5 x 7.5 cm]) with nonstick cooking spray, or use Fold-Your-Own Loaf Pans (page 20).

In a large mixing bowl, combine the flour, salt, cinnamon, baking soda, baking powder, arrowroot, evaporated cane juice, nuts, and raisins.

In a separate bowl using an electric mixer, beat together the oil, mashed banana, and vanilla. Add to the flour mixture and stir to combine, taking care not to overmix.

Fill each loaf tin just under half full.

Bake for 40 to 50 minutes, or until a knife inserted into the center of the crown comes out clean and the bread is dark golden brown. If you are using mini loaf tins, bake for 45–60 minutes.

Let cool completely before turning out the loaves.

YIELD: 5 mini or 2 standard loaves

Gift It!

Wrap in plastic wrap or place in cellophane bags and attach a cute Label (pages 30–31) or tie on a pretty ribbon with a Hang Tag (pages 30–33).

Choconut Mounds

Growing up, I was one of those weird kids who actually loved coconut, and Almond Joys were one of my favorite candy bars. I think the flavor of these is very reminiscent of that candy. The nuts are optional, because, if I recall, "Sometimes you feel like a nut, and sometimes you don't!"

1 cup (224 g) nondairy butter

1 cup (200 g) evaporated cane juice or sugar

1 (14-ounce, or 396 g) package sweetened shredded coconut flakes

1 tablespoon (15 ml) vanilla extract

⅓ cup (30 g) sliced or slivered almonds (optional)

1 cup (176 g) nondairy chocolate chips

Line a baking sheet with parchment or waxed paper.

In a saucepot, melt the butter and evaporated cane juice over medium heat until the sugar is dissolved and the mixture just begins to bubble. Stir in the coconut and cook, stirring constantly, until the coconut is lightly browned and toasted, about 5 minutes. Remove from the heat and stir in the vanilla, almonds, and chocolate chips until completely melted.

Form into 40 balls using about 1 tablespoon (28 g) of dough, place on the prepared baking sheet, and allow to cool completely before packaging.

YIELD: 40 balls

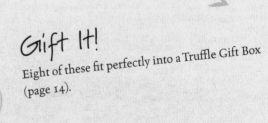

Gift It!

Eight of these fit perfectly into a Truffle Gift Box (page 14).

Cake Truffles

So, if you and I were hanging out and you asked me, "How do you make cake truffles?" I would say to you, "I just smash cake with frosting, and dip it in chocolate." But, because this is a cookbook, I suppose I should be more specific. (Seriously, though, smash cake with frosting and dip it in chocolate!)

9-inch (23 cm) single layer cake (recipe follows, or use your favorite cake)

1 cup (300 g) frosting (recipe follows, or use your favorite frosting)

1 cup (176 g) vegan white or dark chocolate chips or candy coating (recipe follows)

30 mini baking cups

30 Popsicle or lollipop sticks, if making pops

In a mixing bowl, smash the cake with the frosting until well combined and the consistency is moldable. Form into 30 truffle-size balls, place on a baking sheet lined with parchment or waxed paper, and place in the freezer to stiffen.

Melt the chocolate in a double boiler. (If you do not have a double boiler, you can use a metal mixing bowl on top of a pot of water.)

Roll the balls in the chocolate, using a spoon to coat, and place back on the baking sheet to harden. If desired, you can decorate with nuts, crushed candies, or sprinkles.

Once completely hardened, place in the mini baking cups, and press the sticks into the center of the balls to make cake pops.

YIELD: 30 truffles

Plain Vanilla Cake

Here is a plain vanilla cake perfect for making Cake Truffles.

3 cups (375 g) all-purpose flour

1 teaspoon baking soda

1 teaspoon baking powder

¼ teaspoon salt

6 ounces (170 g) vanilla or plain nondairy yogurt

1 cup (200 g) sugar

¼ cup (60 ml) canola oil

2 tablespoons (30 ml) vanilla extract

Preheat the oven to 350°F (180°C, or gas mark 4). Lightly coat a 9-inch (23 cm) cake pan with nonstick spray.

In a mixing bowl, combine the flour, baking soda, baking powder, and salt.

In a separate bowl, mix together the yogurt, sugar, oil, and vanilla. Fold into the flour mixture, being careful not to overmix. Pour evenly into the prepared cake pan.

Bake for 25 to 30 minutes, or until a toothpick inserted into the center comes out clean.

Allow to cool completely.

YIELD: One 9-inch (23 cm) cake

Simple Fluffy Frosting

Here is a simple frosting to use when making Cake Truffles.

½ cup (112 g) nondairy butter

½ cup (96 g) shortening

1 teaspoon vanilla extract

2 cups (240 g) powdered sugar

With an electric mixer, beat together the butter, shortening, and vanilla until creamy. Add the powdered sugar and beat until fluffy.

YIELD: 1½ cups (450 g)

Variations: To make cream cheese frosting, replace the butter and shortening with 1 cup (240 g) nondairy cream cheese. To make chocolate frosting, add ¼ cup (20 g) cocoa powder.

White Chocolate Candy Coating

White chocolate? Yep, it exists. Just not in any store around here.
Sure, you can order vegan white chocolate chips online, but I am not so patient,
so I make my own white chocolate candy coating.

4 ounces (114 g) food-grade cocoa butter

1 cup (120 g) powdered sugar

Melt the cocoa butter in a double boiler, then add the powdered sugar and stir until smooth.

Use as you would any melted chocolate, for dipping and drizzling.

YIELD: 1 cup (235 ml)

Gift It!

Eight truffles fit into a Truffle Gift Box (page 14) quite nicely!

Peanut Butter Balls

Who doesn't love peanut butter and chocolate?
These balls take a little more time to make, but the result is not
only a great gift, but a delicious one as well.

- 1 cup (256 g) no-stir creamy peanut butter
- 1 cup (120 g) powdered sugar
- 12 ounces (340 g) vegan chocolate chips
- 16 toothpicks

In a mixing bowl, knead together the peanut butter and powdered sugar until a nice smooth dough is formed with the consistency of playdough. You may need a little more or a little less sugar depending on the moisture content of your peanut butter.

Form into 16 balls using about 1 tablespoon (21 g) of dough, place on a baking sheet lined with parchment or waxed paper, stick a toothpick into each ball, and place in the freezer to harden. (This step makes it easier to dip them into the chocolate.)

While the balls are freezing, melt the chocolate in a double boiler. Dip each ball into the chocolate to coat, and return to the baking sheet.

Carefully remove the toothpicks. Using the flat side of a butter knife, carefully smooth over the hole where the toothpick was removed, adding a swirl design if desired.

Once completely cooled and hardened, package in candy-size baking cups and place in a truffle box.

YIELD: 16 balls

Gift It!

Eight balls fit perfectly inside a homemade Truffle Gift Box (page 14), so this recipe yields two gifts. (That is, if you don't eat them yourself!)

Saltine Butter Toffee

This is one of those recipes that I think everyone has in his or her stash. But guess what? It makes a great gift, and it is super yummy. This is my version. There is just no way that anyone would ever suspect the vegan-ocity here. They are too buttery and delicious. Feel free to experiment and play with different toppings, such as sprinkles, crushed candy canes, or even coarse sea salt.

35 to 40 saltine crackers

1 cup (224 g) nondairy butter

1 cup (200 g) evaporated cane juice or sugar

2 cups (352 g) vegan chocolate chips

1 cup (120 g) chopped nuts (any nut will do!)

Preheat the oven to 350°F (180°C, or gas mark 4). Line a rimmed baking sheet with aluminum foil, and spray lightly with nonstick spray. Lay the crackers on the sheet in a single layer.

In a saucepot over medium heat, melt the butter and evaporated cane juice until completely dissolved. Pour evenly over the crackers.

Bake for 10 to 12 minutes, until golden.

Carefully remove from the oven. Place on a flat surface, and immediately sprinkle the chocolate chips evenly all over the crackers. Using a spreader or butter knife, spread the chocolate evenly over the crackers as it melts. Sprinkle with the nuts or other desired toppings.

Allow to cool and harden completely before breaking into pieces and packaging for gifts.

YIELD: 35 to 40 pieces

Gift It!

Package several shards in a Window Treat Box (page 16) or in a Truffle Gift Box (page 14), as shown.

Chocolate Bark

Let's face it, almost anything tastes fabulous when it's mixed with chocolate. Bark lets you get creative with your mix-ins. Who knows, maybe you will come up with the next crazy food combo!

12 ounces (340 g) vegan chocolate chips

2 ounces (58 g) food-grade paraffin wax, such as Parowax (optional)

1 tablespoon (15 ml) flavored extract of your choice (see below)

2 cups (250 g) crushed mix-ins (see below), divided

Some of my favorite combos are:

- Crushed pretzels and vanilla extract

- Crushed candy canes and peppermint extract

- Smoked almonds and liquid smoke

- Candied Citrus Peel (page 68) and orange extract

- Mixed nuts and almond extract

- Chopped-up marshmallows (don't mix with the chocolate, just arrange on the baking sheet and pour the chocolate over them, then sprinkle extra on top) and vanilla extract

- Crushed chocolate cookies (such as Oreos) and vanilla extract

- Homemade vegan bacon bits and liquid smoke

- Pumpkin seeds and 1 teaspoon chipotle powder

Line a rimmed baking sheet with parchment.

Place the chocolate and wax (if using) in a double boiler, and melt over medium heat, stirring until smooth. If you don't have a double boiler, just do as I do, and place a metal mixing bowl over a pot of water. Take care not to get water in your melting chocolate.

Just before you are ready to pour the chocolate, stir in the flavored extract. If you are not using the wax, you need to add your extract before melting the chocolate. Adding it after it is already melted can cause it to seize. Add half of the mix-ins and stir to combine.

Pour the chocolate evenly onto the baking sheet. Sprinkle the remaining mix-ins evenly all over the top.

Allow to cool and harden completely before breaking into pieces and packaging for gifting.

YIELD: 24 ounces (672 g)

Note: If you want to take it to the next level, repeat the process, following the same instructions above, this time with vegan white chocolate, and pour it directly over the first batch after it hardens. You will have two layers, one dark and one white!

Cooking with Wax

Have you ever cooked with wax—food-grade paraffin wax, that is? I use it in my barks for a few reasons:

1. To prevent bloom. Good, real, chocolate will get a white coating on top after a few days if the chocolate was not tempered properly, and I have a tough time ever getting my chocolate to temper properly.

2. It makes the chocolate shiny.

3. It thins out the chocolate while it is hot. You can actually add a bit to the Peanut Butter Balls (page 63) to make the dipping process easier. In fact, add a small amount to any "chocolate-dipped" recipe to make it easier to work with.

I use Parowax, or food-grade paraffin (which can usually be found in the baking or canning aisle of your grocery store) in this recipe. But it is totally optional, and you can leave it out if you want to. It will not affect the flavor of the candy either way.

Candied Citrus Peel

This recipe makes good use of the part of the fruit most people throw in the compost heap! The recipe uses two average-size navel oranges, but any citrus fruit can be used. If your fruit has a rather thick pith, scrape away most of it, as it can remain bitter, even after candying. A little bit is okay, but you just don't want a big, thick layer of the stuff, you know? You can kick these up a notch by dipping them halfway into chocolate as a luxurious option ... mmmm, dark chocolate and orange. So yummy. Another really cool thing about these is that the syrup left over after you simmer the rinds is a very flavorful simple syrup that tastes great in a cocktail, or to sweeten your tea, and you can even use it in baking applications!

2 medium ripe navel oranges

3 cups (600 g) evaporated cane juice or sugar, divided

1 cup (235 ml) water

1 teaspoon vanilla extract

Cut the oranges into quarters and peel away the flesh. (You can snack on the flesh while boiling the rinds, or save it for another use.) Cut the rind into long julienne strips, about ¼ inch (6 mm) thick and the length of the orange.

Add 2 cups (400 g) of the evaporated cane juice and the water to a saucepot with a tight-fitting lid. Bring to a boil over medium-high, then reduce to a simmer. Add the peels and stir to coat. Stir in the vanilla.

Cover and simmer for 30 minutes, stirring occasionally to make sure the rinds are not stuck to the bottom or to each other.

Place the remaining 1 cup (200 g) sugar in a shallow dish.

Using tongs, pick up a few of the rinds out of the syrup and allow the excess syrup to drain off. Place them in the sugar and toss to completely coat.

Place in a single layer on a plate or tray to cool completely before packaging. Don't forget to reserve that sweet syrup for a later use!

YIELD: About 48 pieces

Gift It!

I like to package these up in cellophane bags with a cute little Hang Tag (pages 30–33) or sticker Labels (pages 30–31), but they serve up just as nicely in Double Pocket Gift Bags (page 13) or Super Simple Gift Envelopes (page 12), especially if you make several flavors.

Old-Fashioned Mashed Potato Candy

Yep. Candy made from mashed potatoes. Actually, there is so much sugar in these, no one would ever guess that you made them from mashed potatoes. This is an old family recipe that has been passed down for generations. It's naturally vegan, so no substitutes were necessary. Plus, it's a fun way to use up your leftover mashers. For years, my mom and I have been making it according to the following recipe: "Mix powdered sugar with mashed potato to form a dough. Roll out dough and spread on peanut butter. Roll up and slice." That really is all you need to know. You can use instant mashed potatoes for these, too. This batch uses almost 6 pounds (2.7 kg) of powdered sugar.

3 cups (227 g) dehydrated potato flakes

2 cups (470 ml) water

1 cup (235 ml) vanilla or plain soy milk

6 pounds (2.7 kg) powdered sugar, divided

½ cup (128 g) peanut butter, for spreading

In a large mixing bowl, add the potato flakes. Bring the water and soy milk to a boil in a saucepot over high heat. As soon as it begins to boil, remove from the heat and mix into the potato flakes. Stir well, and allow to cool. Add the powdered sugar, 1 cup (120 g) at a time (6 pounds [2.7 kg] equals roughly 23 cups [2.7 kg]), beating with an electric mixer after each addition. As the "dough" begins to thicken, you will have to abandon the mixer and knead with your hands. Keep adding sugar until your dough is workable and no longer sticky. Once you achieve a workable dough, divide it into 10 pieces.

On a well-sugared surface, roll out one piece at a time. Spread on the peanut butter. Roll it up. Slice into saltwater taffy–size pieces.

Wrap in waxed paper squares for an old-fashioned look and to easily package for gift giving.

YIELD: 200 pieces

Note: Recipe tester Kelly Cavalier added black licorice to the center and shredded coconut to her potatoes! GENIUS! Just like the coconut rolls in a package of Licorice Allsorts.

Gift It!

Wrap each piece individually in a square of waxed paper, and twist the ends to seal. Package in pretty Window Treat Boxes (page 16) or Double Pocket Gift Bags (page 13), and add a pretty Hang Tag (pages 30–33).

Sea Salt Caramels

Full disclosure here: The original inspiration for this recipe came from Ina Garten's recipe on the Food Network website. After several tries, using varying versions, and varying amounts of the same ingredients, the following vegan recipe was developed.

2 cups (400 g) evaporated cane juice or granulated sugar

½ cup (120 ml) light corn syrup

½ cup (120 ml) water

½ cup (112 g) nondairy butter such as Earth Balance

2 cups (470 ml) MimicCreme

½ teaspoon fine sea salt

1 teaspoon vanilla extract

Coarse sea salt, for sprinkling

Gift It!

Package in pretty Window Treat Boxes (page 16) or Reusable Felt Gift Bags (page 18), adding a pretty Hang Tag (pages 30–33).

Line an 8 x 8-inch (20 x 20 cm) square pan or dish with two pieces of parchment paper, one going in each direction, with plenty of overhang, so that you can easily lift the caramel out of the dish once it is cool. Lightly brush the paper with vegetable oil, or spray lightly with nonstick spray.

You will need a deep pot (this is very important because the mixture can boil up violently, and a sticky sugary boil-over can be both dangerous and a real pain to clean up!). I suggest a soup pot at least 8 inches (20 cm) deep. Attach a candy thermometer to the side and add the evaporated cane juice, corn syrup, and water. Stir to combine and bring to a boil over medium-high heat.

While the sugar is coming to a boil, add the butter, cream, and fine sea salt to a smaller saucepot. Bring to a simmer over medium-high heat.

Timing is key. The goal is to get the butter and cream to simmer just as your sugar mixture is turning a golden amber color and boiling at about 200°F (93°C). Should the butter and cream begin to simmer before the sugar is ready, simply lower the heat or remove it from the heat and set aside.

When the sugar mixture is ready, carefully and slowly stir the butter cream mixture into the boiling sugar mixture using a wooden spoon (wood does not conduct heat the same way as metal). IT WILL BOIL UP VIOLENTLY!

Once all of the crazy boiling settles down, continue to boil the mixture, stirring occasionally, until it reaches the firm-ball stage, or 248°F (120°C). Remove from the heat, and stir in the vanilla with a wooden spoon.

Carefully pour the mixture into the lined pan or dish and smooth out the excess bubbles with the back of the wooden spoon.

Allow to cool before slicing into 1-inch (2.5 cm) squares.

Press a small pinch of coarse sea salt into the top of each square. Wrap each candy in a 4-inch (10 cm) square of waxed paper and twist the ends closed.

YIELD: 64 candies

Candied Nuts

Who doesn't love nuts? I like to use pecans, walnuts, cashews, and almonds in this mix, but feel free to use any combo of your favorite nuts. This is actually two recipes, but the directions are the same for both. Just decide whether you want to make your batch sweet or spicy and then follow the ingredients list for that type.

For Nut Mix:

1 cup (120 g) pecan halves

1 cup (120 g) walnut halves

1 cup (120 g) whole cashews

1 cup (120 g) whole almonds

For Sweet Blend:

½ cup (110 g) firmly packed brown sugar

¼ cup (56 g) nondairy butter, melted

½ teaspoon ground cinnamon

¼ teaspoon salt

¼ teaspoon ground nutmeg

¼ teaspoon ground cloves

For Spicy Blend:

½ cup (110 g) firmly packed brown sugar

¼ cup (56 g) nondairy butter, melted

½ teaspoon cayenne pepper (or to taste)

¼ teaspoon smoked paprika

¼ teaspoon salt

To make the nut mix: Preheat the oven to 400°F (200°C, or gas mark 6). Line a baking sheet with parchment.

In a mixing bowl, combine the nuts.

To make either the sweet or the spicy blend: In a small bowl mix together the blend ingredients of your choice.

Toss together the nuts with the blend mix until all the nuts are coated. Spread evenly in a layer on the baking sheet. Bake for 8 to 10 minutes, checking often to prevent burning, turning as necessary.

Remove from the oven and allow to cool completely before breaking apart and packaging.

YIELD: 3 ½ cups (420 g)

Gift It!

Package them up in cellophane bags, brown paper bags, tins, jars, canisters, or boxes. As long as you affix a nice Label (pages 30–31), they'll be a hit!

Twigs and Berries

Because vegans only eat twigs and berries, why not show those omnis how tasty they can be? Below are two versions, sweet and spicy, based on the same basic mix. This recipe makes a HUGE amount. I use this one when I am making lots of gifts. Feel free to cut the recipe in half, especially if you don't have an industrial-size mixing bowl.

For Base Mix:

7 cups (216 g) crunchy rice square cereal, such as Rice Chex

3 cups (112 g) pretzel sticks

1 cup (142 g) dried cranberries

1 cup (160 g) raisins

1 cup (84 g) banana chips

1 cup (124 g) raw pepitas (pumpkin seeds)

1 cup (112 g) each raw almonds and pecans

To make the base mix: In your largest mixing bowl, toss together all the ingredients, then follow the instructions for either the sweet or the spicy version below (or do one half of each).

Allow to cool completely then package in clear bags, tins, or jars and make sure to add a Hang Tag (pages 30–33).

For Sweet Mix:

2 cups (352 g) nondairy semisweet chocolate chips

1 cup (224 g) nondairy butter

½ cup (128 g) creamy no-stir peanut butter

2 teaspoons ground cinnamon

2 teaspoons vanilla extract

5 to 6 cups (600 to 720 g) powdered sugar, divided

To make the sweet mix: In a saucepot over low heat, melt the chocolate chips, butter, and peanut butter. Stir in the cinnamon and vanilla. Pour the mixture over the base mix and stir to coat evenly.

Add the powdered sugar, 1 cup (120 g) at a time, and toss to coat. By the time you add the last cup of sugar, your mix should be powdery white and the pieces should not stick together.

Allow to cool (you can leave it right in the bowl) before packaging.

For Spicy Mix:

2 cups (448 g) nondairy butter

½ cup (120 ml) soy sauce or tamari

2 tablespoons (30 ml) sriracha

2 tablespoons (16 g) garlic powder

2 tablespoons (16 g) onion powder

2 teaspoons ground black pepper

2 teaspoons paprika

2 teaspoons red pepper flakes

1 teaspoon ground chipotle powder or cayenne pepper (or to taste)

To make the spicy mix: Preheat the oven to 250°F (120°C, or gas mark ½). Line 4 baking pans with parchment.

In a saucepot over low heat, add all the ingredients and stir until completely melted. Pour the mixture over the base mix and toss until evenly coated. Spread evenly in a single layer on the baking sheets.

Bake for 45 minutes to 1 hour, or until crisp.

Allow to cool completely before packaging.

YIELD: 16 cups (1.4 kg)

Cowgirl Blackening Rub

Inspired by the deep nuanced notes in mole, a traditional sauce made from a plethora of herbs, spices, chocolate, coffee, and many other ingredients that can take hours to make...this mix is a good stand-in when I crave these flavors.

2 tablespoons (16 g) chili powder

1 tablespoon (6 g) ground black pepper

1 tablespoon (18 g) sea salt

1 tablespoon (8 g) granulated garlic

1 tablespoon (8 g) onion powder

1 tablespoon (7 g) smoked paprika

2 teaspoons ground mustard seed

1 teaspoon instant coffee crystals

1 teaspoon evaporated cane juice

1 teaspoon red pepper flakes

½ teaspoon unsweetened cocoa powder

⅛ teaspoon ground cloves

Mix all the ingredients together until well combined.

YIELD: ¾ cup (108 g)

Gift It!

Package in a shaker or a jar and attach a Hang Tag (pages 30–33) or Label (pages 30–31) that reads, "Cowgirl Blackening Rub: This spice mix works great as a dry rub on tofu, tempeh, or seitan, or mixed with olive oil to make a marinade for veggies. It also tastes great blended with eggless mayonnaise to make a kicky aioli, or try simmering it with tomato sauce for an almost instant mole."

Trabuco Canyon Magic Dust

This recipe was developed by Karen Balthaser at the Big "B" Ranch here in Trabuco Canyon, California. It yields a huge batch so you can make lots of gifts at once. Feel free to cut it down as needed. Karen also says you can fuss around with the amounts to suit your taste.

2 cups (576 g) salt

2 cups (256 g) granulated garlic

¾ cup (72 g) ground black pepper

¾ cup (96 g) onion powder

½ cup (56 g) cayenne pepper

¼ cup (24 g) ground white pepper

2 tablespoons (13 g) celery seed

2 tablespoons (4 g) dried parsley flakes, finely ground in a coffee grinder

Mix all the ingredients together in a mixing bowl until well combined.

Package in a spice shaker or jar with a Hang Tag (pages 30–33) that reads [insert your name or town here] Magic Dust. This special seasoning is great for grilling, as a rub, or any way you please. For a quick and easy side dish, toss with potatoes or veggies. Sauté in olive oil.

YIELD: 6 ½ cups (1.1 kg)

Groovy Granola

If eating granola promotes peace on Earth, free love, and happiness,
well, then, pour me another bowl, man! Package this up in cellophane bags
tied up all pretty-like with a bow and a cute hang tag.

For Snack Version:

1 cup (99 g) pecans

½ cup (60 g) shredded coconut
    (sweetened or unsweetened)

2 cups (164 g) old-fashioned rolled oats

1 teaspoon ground cinnamon

¼ teaspoon sea salt

½ cup (120 ml) agave nectar

1 teaspoon vanilla extract

¼ cup (56 g) nondairy butter, melted, or
    vegetable oil

½ cup (61 g) dried cranberries

½ cup (88 g) white or dark vegan
    chocolate chips

To make the snack version: Preheat the oven to 300°F (150°C, or gas mark 2). Line a rimmed baking sheet with parchment or a silicone baking mat.

Preheat a large dry frying pan over medium heat. Add the pecans and coconut and toast lightly, tossing constantly.

Combine the toasted mixture, oats, cinnamon, and salt in a large bowl.

Mix together the agave, vanilla, and melted butter in a small bowl. Add to the oat mixture and toss to coat. Transfer the mixture to baking sheet and spread in a single layer.

Bake for 30 minutes, returning every 10 minutes to turn with a spatula to make sure the whole batch gets browned evenly. Remove from the oven and allow to cool.

Return the mixture to the bowl and mix in the cranberries and chocolate chips, breaking up any large clumps.

YIELD: 1 ½ pounds (680 g)

For Breakfast Version:

2 cups (164 g) old-fashioned rolled oats

½ cup (45 g) sliced almonds

½ teaspoon ground cinnamon

¼ teaspoon sea salt

½ cup (120 ml) agave nectar

1 teaspoon vanilla extract

¼ cup (56 g) nondairy butter, melted, or
    vegetable oil

1 cup (14 g) freeze-dried blueberries

To make the breakfast version: Preheat the oven to 300°F (150°C, or gas mark 2). Line a rimmed baking sheet with parchment or a silicone baking mat.

Combine the oats, almonds, cinnamon, and salt in a mixing bowl.

Mix together the agave, vanilla, and melted butter in a small bowl. Add to the oat mixture and toss to coat. Transfer the mixture to the baking sheet and spread in a single layer.

Bake for 30 minutes, returning every 10 minutes to turn with a spatula to make sure the whole batch gets browned evenly. Remove from the oven and allow to cool.

Return the mixture to the bowl and mix in the dried blueberries, breaking up any large clumps.

YIELD: 1 pound (454 g)

Minty
Doggie
Biscuits

Minty Doggie Biscuits

Four-legged friends like vegan food gifts, too!
This recipe is courtesy of my awesome-rad-übercool mom. She makes these
for my three girls every Christmas. My girls love their Gramma Kim.

1 tablespoon (15 ml) vegetable oil

1 cup (235 ml) water

2 ½ cups (300 g) whole wheat flour

½ cup (39 g) quick-cooking oats

⅓ cup (20 g) finely chopped fresh mint

⅓ cup (20 g) finely chopped fresh parsley

Preheat the oven to 325°F (170°C, or gas mark 3). Line a baking sheet with parchment or a silicone baking mat.

In a medium mixing bowl, combine the oil and water. Slowly add the flour, oats, mint, and parsley and mix until well combined.

Turn the dough out onto a floured surface and roll out to ¼ inch (6 mm) thick. Cut into fun shapes with cookie cutters.

Bake for 35 minutes, turning them halfway through to make sure they don't brown too much on one side. Let cool before packaging.

YIELD: About 2 dozen biscuits depending on the size of your cookie cutter

Gift It!

Wrap in cellophane bags, Super Simple Gift Envelopes (page 12), or Window Treat Boxes (page 16) tied up with pretty ribbons with an attached card that reads, "The fresh flavor of parsley and mint helps freshen a doggie's breath. Mint can also be soothing to the stomach and nervous system, while parsley can help with joint pain."

To:

From:

Chapter 3

Just Add Water

Make-at-Home Gift Mixes for Anytime Assembly

This chapter is full of recipes for "make-it-yourself" gifts that your "giftee" can assemble whenever they choose. There are cookie and cake mixes layered into mason jars like the sand art of decades past. You'll also find soup mixes, hot and cold drink mixes, and even a mix for instant mac and cheese. One of the best things about the gifts in this chapter is the shelf life. So often we give baked goods as gifts, but baked goods need to be gifted and consumed right away. These, on the other hand, can be made ahead of time, and the receiver can save them for the perfect occasion to prepare.

Instant Sweet Lemon Iced Tea Mix

This instant iced tea mix is a perfect host or hostess gift when attending a summertime barbecue or get-together. The ingredients are simple, and it is a snap to throw together in a hurry.

2 cups (67 g) unsweetened instant 100% tea crystals (the only ingredient on the label should be tea)

3 cups (600 g) evaporated cane juice

2 (⅓-ounce, or 9 g each) packets unsweetened lemonade drink mix or 2 tablespoons (18 g) citric acid

Zest of 2 lemons

Combine all the ingredients together in a mixing bowl.

YIELD: 4 cups (896 g) mix

Gift It!

This refreshing tea packs well in mason jars, cellophane bags, and individual Double Pocket Gift Bags (page 13) made with 8 ½ x 11-inch (21.5 x 28 cm) sheets of paper. Be sure to add the recipe card at right.

Sweet Lemon Iced Tea

- To make 1 cup (235 ml): Combine 2 tablespoons (28 g) mix with 1 cup (235 ml) warm water.

- To make 1 quart (1 L): Combine ½ cup (112 g) mix with 4 cups (1 L) warm water.

- To make ½ gallon (2 L): Combine 1 cup (224 g) mix with 8 cups (1.8 L) warm water.

- To make 1 gallon (4 L): Combine 2 cups (448 g) mix with 16 cups (3.8 L) warm water.

- Chill before serving.

Contents: 4 cups (896 g) mix

Instant Mocha Mix

Think International Café, but vegan, all natural, homemade, and not made by Maxwell House. If you can't get your hands on powdered rice milk, just leave it out, but be sure to change the instructions to use nondairy milk instead of water. If you can't find instant espresso, you can substitute instant coffee crystals, but double the amount.

1 cup (80 g) cocoa powder

1 cup (120 g) powdered sugar

½ cup (92 g) powdered rice milk

½ cup (40 g) instant espresso powder

Combine all the ingredients together in a mixing bowl.

YIELD: 3 cups (332 g) mix

Gift It!

Package in glass jars, a small Double Pocket Gift Bag (page 13), cellophane bags, or a cellophane bag tucked into a mug. Be sure to add the recipe card at right.

Instant Mocha

Just add water!

Combine 2 heaping tablespoons (14 g) mix with 1 cup (235 ml) boiling water. For an extra-special treat, top with nondairy whipped topping or a sprinkling of cinnamon.

Contents: 3 cups (332 g) mix

Fudgy Brownie Mix

This mix yields a super fudgy brownie. And it's way, way better than a store-bought mix because it's made with love.

½ cup (110 g) firmly packed brown sugar

1 ½ cups (188 g) all-purpose flour

½ teaspoon baking soda

½ teaspoon baking powder

½ teaspoon salt

½ cup (40 g) unsweetened cocoa

1 cup (200 g) evaporated cane juice or granulated sugar

1 cup (176 g) vegan semisweet chocolate chips

Layer the ingredients in a quart-size (1 L) jar in the order listed.

YIELD: 9 brownies

Fudgy Brownies

- 1 jar Fudgy Brownie Mix
- ¾ cup (180 ml) nondairy milk
- ⅓ cup (80 ml) vegetable oil
- ⅓ cup (113 g) applesauce
- 2 teaspoons vanilla extract

Preheat the oven to 350°F (180°C, or gas mark 4). Line a 9 x 9-inch (23 x 23 cm) baking dish with parchment. Remove the chocolate chips from the top of the brownie mix jar and set aside. Empty the remaining contents of the jar into a mixing bowl and stir until well combined. In a small saucepot, bring the milk to a boil. As soon as it begins to boil, add the chocolate chips and stir until completely melted. Remove from the heat and stir in the oil, applesauce, and vanilla. Add to the dry ingredients and stir until well combined. Pour the batter into the prepared baking dish and bake for 35 to 40 minutes, or until a toothpick inserted into the center comes out clean. Remove from the oven and allow to cool completely. Once cool, cut into squares and enjoy.

Yield: 9 brownies

Gift It!

Tie on the recipe card with a pretty ribbon or twine.

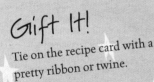

Double Chocolate Chip Cookie Mix

Chocolate chip cookies are good. Chocolate chocolate chip cookies are even better!

- 1 ½ cups (187 g) all-purpose flour
- ¼ cup (32 g) arrowroot powder or cornstarch
- ½ teaspoon baking soda
- ¼ teaspoon salt
- ½ cup (40 g) unsweetened cocoa powder
- ¾ cup (75 g) evaporated cane juice or granulated sugar
- ⅓ cup (73 g) firmly packed brown sugar
- 2 cups (352 g) vegan chocolate chips

Layer all the ingredients in a jar, or mix all the ingredients together until well combined and place in a plastic bag.

YIELD: 3 dozen cookies

Double Chocolate Chip Cookies

- ¾ cup (180 ml) canola or other mild-flavored vegetable oil
- ½ cup (120 ml) nondairy milk
- 1 ½ teaspoons vanilla extract
- Double Chocolate Chip Cookie Mix

Preheat the oven to 350°F (180°C, or gas mark 4). Line 2 or 3 baking sheets with parchment or silicone mats.

In a large mixing bowl, combine the oil, milk, and vanilla. Add the cookie mix and stir until well combined.

Drop 2 heaping tablespoons (about 40 g) of dough onto the baking sheets about 2 inches (5 cm) apart. Bake for 15 to 20 minutes, or until the edges begin to lift.

Allow to cool for 5 minutes on the baking sheet before transferring to a rack to cool completely.

Yield: 3 dozen cookies

Gift It!

You can layer this in a jar, but it requires a large jar, so I generally mix all of the ingredients and gift it in a bag. You can go simple, and just place it into a cellophane bag and tie on the recipe instructions, or get a bit fancier and make your own cookie mix packaging. Place the mix in a cellophane bag, and seal. Then place the bag inside a Super Simple Gift Envelope (page 12) and apply a Label (pages 30–31) to the front of the envelope saying what is inside, then add the instructions to a label on the back.

Blueberry Oatmeal Chocolate Chip Cookie Mix

Freeze-dried blueberries make this mix not-your-typical-cookie-mix-in-a-jar.

1 cup (220 g) lightly packed brown sugar

1 cup (172 g) vegan chocolate chips

1 cup (125 g) all-purpose flour

½ teaspoon baking soda

½ teaspoon baking powder

¼ teaspoon salt

1 cup (14 g) freeze-dried blueberries

1 cup (78 g) quick-cooking oats

Layer the ingredients in a quart-size (1 L) jar in the order listed.

YIELD: 2 dozen cookies

Blueberry Oatmeal Chocolate Chip Cookies

- 1 jar Blueberry Oatmeal Chocolate Chip Cookie Mix
- ½ cup (112 g) nondairy butter, melted
- 6 ounces (170 g) plain nondairy yogurt
- 1 tablespoon (15 ml) vanilla extract

Preheat the oven to 350°F (180°C, or gas mark 4). Line 2 baking sheets with parchment or silicone baking mat.

Empty the contents of the jar into a mixing bowl and stir until well combined.

In a separate bowl, mix together the melted butter, yogurt, and vanilla. Add to the dry ingredients and stir until well incorporated.

Spoon a heaping 2 tablespoons (about 50 g) of dough onto the baking sheets, leaving at least 2 inches (5 cm) between cookies on the sheet. Bake for 12 to 15 minutes, or until golden brown around the edges.

Allow to cool for 5 minutes before transferring to a wire rack to cool completely.

Yield: 2 dozen cookies

Gift It!

Attach the recipe card to the jar with a pretty ribbon or twine.

Strawberry Pineapple Orange Cake Mix

Some of the most awesome mixes can be made with all of the amazing dried fruits and vegetables available these days. They retain their bright colors and flavors, which makes them extra pretty and delicious in these mixes. The freeze-dried fruits and vegetables that I use come from Justtomatoes.com. If you do not have vanilla powder, leave it out of the mix, but be sure to add "2 teaspoons vanilla extract" to the ingredients (and directions) on the recipe card.

2 ½ cups (313 g) all-purpose flour

1 cup (200 g) evaporated cane juice or granulated sugar

2 tablespoons (16 g) cornstarch

2 teaspoons baking powder

2 teaspoons vanilla powder

1 teaspoon baking soda

½ teaspoon sea salt

1 cup (20 g) freeze-dried strawberries

½ cup (10 g) freeze-dried pineapple

Layer the ingredients in a quart-size (1 L) plastic bag in the order listed.

YIELD: One 8- or 9-inch (20 or 23 cm) single-layer cake

Strawberry Pineapple Orange Cake

- 1 bag Strawberry Pineapple Orange Cake Mix
- 1 cup (235 ml) soy, almond, or coconut milk
- 1 cup (235 ml) orange juice
- ¼ cup (60 ml) canola or other mild-flavored vegetable oil

Preheat the oven to 350°F (180°C, or gas mark 4). Lightly coat an 8-inch (20 cm)-square or 9-inch (23 cm)-round cake pan with nonstick spray.

Empty the contents of the bag into a mixing bowl and stir until well combined. Add the milk, orange juice, and oil and stir until well combined. Pour the batter into the cake pan.

Bake for 50 to 60 minutes, until golden and a toothpick inserted into the center comes out clean. Allow to cool completely before inverting the pan onto a cake platter.

Top with a simple icing of ½ cup (60 g) powdered sugar mixed with 2 tablespoons (30 ml) orange juice, if desired.

Yield: One 8- or 9-inch (20 or 23 cm) cake

Gift It!
Tie closed with a pretty ribbon or twine, and attach the recipe card at right.

Brown Sugar and Cinnamon Oatmeal with Raisins Mix

I love the idea of a wholesome, delicious, hearty hot breakfast that can be made in less than five minutes. This is a perfect gift for anyone you know that has a busy schedule.

2 cups (156 g) quick-cooking oats

½ cup (110 g) firmly packed brown sugar

½ cup (80 g) raisins

½ teaspoon ground cinnamon

½ teaspoon salt

Layer the ingredients in a pint-size (470 g) jar in the order listed.

YIELD: 6 servings

Brown Sugar Oatmeal with Raisins

Just add water!

Per serving: Combine ½ cup (58 g) mix with 1 cup (235 ml) boiling water, nondairy milk, or apple cider. Stir, cover, and let stand for 1 minute before enjoying.

To make in the microwave: Mix ½ cup (58 g) mix with 1 cup (235 ml) boiling water, nondairy milk, or apple cider and cook for 1½ to 2 minutes. Stir well before serving.

Yield: 6 servings

Gift It!

Tie on the recipe card to the jar with a pretty ribbon or twine.

Sweet Cornbread Muffin Mix

These home-style muffins are slightly sweet and crumbly, and taste great warm right out of the oven smothered in nondairy butter and drizzled with agave nectar. They also make a great accompaniment to your favorite chili.

2 cups (250 g) all-purpose flour

1 ½ cups (210 g) yellow cornmeal

½ cup (100 g) evaporated cane juice or granulated sugar

2 tablespoons (24 g) baking powder

2 tablespoons (16 g) cornstarch

2 teaspoons sea salt

Layer all the ingredients in a jar, or mix all the ingredients together until well combined and place in a plastic bag.

YIELD: 12 to 16 muffins

Sweet Cornbread Muffins

- 1 jar Sweet Cornbread Muffin Mix
- 2 cups (470 ml) plain nondairy milk, such as almond, coconut, or soy (rice is not recommended here)
- ½ cup (120 ml) canola or other mild-flavored vegetable oil
- 1 cup (130 g) fresh, frozen, or canned yellow corn kernels (optional)

Preheat the oven to 400°F (200°C, or gas mark 6). Line a standard muffin tin with papers.

Empty the contents of the jar into a mixing bowl and stir to combine. Add the milk and oil and stir until well combined. Stir in the corn, if using.

Distribute the batter evenly among the muffin cups. The cups will be full, which provides for a nice bakery-style top. If you are using corn kernels, or prefer standard-size muffins, fill the cups three-fourths full and your yield will be 16.

Bake for 18 to 20 minutes, or until the tops are golden, firm, and crackly.

Yield: 12 to 16 muffins

Gift It!

Tie on the recipe card to the jar with a pretty ribbon or twine.

Chocolate Chip Pancake Mix

This is an awesome present to give to busy parents because it makes a hot, delicious kid-friendly breakfast in a snap!

2 cups (250 g) all-purpose flour

¼ cup (50 g) sugar

2 tablespoons (24 g) baking powder

2 tablespoons (16 g) cornstarch

1 tablespoon (7 g) flaxseed meal

1 teaspoon salt

1 cup (176 g) vegan chocolate chips

Combine the flour, sugar, baking powder, cornstarch, flaxseed meal, and salt in a bowl and stir to mix. Place in a mason jar or clear plastic bag. Add the chocolate chips on top and seal.

YIELD: 10 to 12 pancakes

Chocolate Chip Pancakes

- 1 jar Chocolate Chip Pancake Mix
- 2 cups (470 ml) vanilla nondairy milk, such as almond, soy, or coconut (rice milk is not recommended here)
- ¼ cup (60 ml) canola or other mild-flavored vegetable oil

Empty the contents of the jar into a large mixing bowl and stir until well combined.
   In a separate small bowl, mix together the milk and oil. Add to the dry ingredients and stir until well combined. Let stand for 5 to 10 minutes.
   Preheat a nonstick skillet or griddle over high heat. Pour about ½ cup (120 ml) of batter onto the skillet. Cook for 2 to 3 minutes, until bubbles begin popping in the batter. Flip over and cook until golden brown on both sides.
   Repeat until all the batter is used.

Yield: 10 to 12 pancakes

Gift It!

Tie on the recipe card to the jar with a pretty ribbon or twine.

Cranberry Muffin Mix

Feel free to change the fruits in this mix to customize it. Instead of cranberries, consider dried blueberries, apples, raisins, pineapple, or even mango! If you do not have vanilla powder, leave it out of the mix, but be sure to add "1 teaspoon vanilla extract" to the ingredients on the recipe card.

- 2 cups (250 g) all-purpose flour
- ½ cup (100 g) sugar
- 2 tablespoons (16 g) cornstarch
- 1 tablespoon (12 g) baking powder
- 1 tablespoon (7 g) flaxseed meal
- 1 teaspoon baking soda
- 1 teaspoon salt
- 1 teaspoon vanilla powder
- ½ teaspoon ground cinnamon
- ¼ teaspoon ground nutmeg
- 1 cup (176 g) dried cranberries
- 1 cup (120 g) chopped walnuts (optional)

Mix everything except the cranberries and nuts together until well combined. Place in a mason jar or clear plastic bag. Add cranberries and nuts to the top and seal.

YIELD: 12 muffins

✂

Cranberry Muffins

These muffins are a great breakfast treat, especially if you top them with a simple icing made from ½ cup (60 g) powdered sugar mixed with 2 tablespoons (30 ml) orange juice.

- 1 jar Cranberry Muffin Mix
- ¼ cup (60 ml) vegetable oil
- 1½ cups (470 ml) vanilla nondairy milk

Preheat the oven to 350°F (180°C, or gas mark 4). Line a standard muffin tin with papers.

Empty the contents of the jar into a mixing bowl and stir to combine. Add the milk and oil and stir until well combined. (Add the vanilla, if using.) Evenly distribute the batter among the cups; the cups will be almost full.

Bake for 18 to 20 minutes, or until golden and a toothpick inserted into the center comes out clean.

Yield: 12 muffins

Gift It!
Tie closed with a pretty ribbon or twine, and attach the recipe card at right.

Southwestern Three-Bean Soup Mix

This soup has some bite due to the addition of dried jalapeño, chipotle powder, and red pepper flakes. Feel free to reduce the heat as needed, although as written it isn't that hot, especially if garnished with nondairy sour cream and avocado.

For Bean Mix:

1 cup (185 g) dry white beans

1 cup (185 g) dry black beans

1 cup (185 g) dry pinto beans

For Seasoning Mix:

¾ cup (72 g) vegetable broth powder

2 tablespoons (15 g) chopped sun-dried tomatoes, not packed in oil

1 tablespoon (4 g) dried jalapeños (optional)

1 tablespoon (8 g) garlic powder

1 tablespoon (8 g) onion powder

1 teaspoon dried parsley

1 teaspoon paprika

1 teaspoon chipotle powder

½ teaspoon red pepper flakes

½ teaspoon ground cumin

½ teaspoon ground black pepper

2 bay leaves

To make the bean mix: Layer the beans in a mason jar.

To make the seasoning mix: Mix together all the seasonings and place in a resealable plastic bag. Place on top of the beans in the jar.

YIELD: 12 servings

Southwestern Three-Bean Soup

Remove the seasoning packet and set aside. Rinse the beans under cold running water.

Add the beans and 8 cups (2 L) water to a large stockpot or Dutch oven with a tight-fitting lid. Bring to a boil over high heat. Reduce the heat to a simmer and cook, uncovered, for 2 minutes. Remove from the heat, cover, and let stand for 1 hour. Drain and rinse the beans. Return the beans to the pot.

Add 12 cups (3 L) fresh water and the seasoning packet. Bring to a boil over high heat, then reduce the heat to a simmer. Simmer, covered, for 75 to 90 minutes, stirring about every 20 minutes, adding more water if needed, until the beans are tender. Discard the bay leaves before serving.

If desired, serve garnished with avocado slices, tortilla chips, and nondairy sour cream.

Yield: 12 servings

Gift It!

To package in a cellophane bag instead of a jar, place the bag of seasonings in the bottom of the bag, then pour the bean mix on top. Be sure to attach the recipe card above with a nice ribbon or bow.

Hearty Pasta Soup with Chik'n Mix

This is a perfect soup to give during cold weather, to a sick friend,
or even just as a friendly anytime gift to warm the soul.

½ cup (48 g) vegetable broth
powder

1 tablespoon (2 g) dried
parsley

1 tablespoon (2 g) dried chives

1 teaspoon onion powder

1 teaspoon dried minced
onion

1 teaspoon dried minced
garlic

½ teaspoon smoked paprika

½ teaspoon dried thyme

½ cup (96 g) dry lentils

2 cups (220 g) tricolor
pasta spirals

1 cup (40 g) Soy Curls or
large chunk TVP

Mix together the vegetable broth powder and all the spices. Place
the spice mix in the bottom of a quart-size jar. Layer the lentils,
pasta, and Soy Curls on top.

YIELD: 6 servings

Hearty Pasta Soup with Chik'n

- 6 cups (1.4 L) water
- 2 tablespoons (30 ml) olive oil (optional)
- 1 jar Hearty Pasta Soup with Chik'n Mix
- Salt and pepper to taste

Add the water and oil to a soup pot with a tight-fitting lid. Bring to a boil over high heat.

Add the entire contents of the jar and stir to combine. Reduce the heat to a simmer, cover, and simmer for 10 to 12 minutes, or until the pasta and lentils are tender.

Yield: 6 servings

Optional add-ins: Peas, diced onion, carrots, and celery make fabulous additions to this already hearty soup.

Gift It!

Tie the recipe card to
the jar with a pretty ribbon
or twine.

Masala Soup Mix

This mix looks so pretty layered in a jar, especially if you use red quinoa and red lentils. So colorful!

1 cup (200 g) red lentils

½ cup (92 g) brown rice

1 cup (196 g) split peas

½ cup (84 g) quinoa

¼ cup (24 g) vegetable broth powder

1 tablespoon (2 g) dried chives

1 teaspoon ground cumin

1 teaspoon coriander

1 teaspoon chili powder

1 teaspoon salt (more or less to taste depending on the saltiness of your broth powder)

½ teaspoon ground cardamom

¼ teaspoon ground cinnamon

¼ teaspoon ground cloves

¼ teaspoon ground nutmeg

¼ teaspoon ground black pepper

1 bay leaf

In a quart-size jar, layer the lentils, rice, peas, and quinoa. In a small bowl, mix together the broth powder and spices and place in a resealable plastic bag. Place on top of the quinoa and seal the jar.

YIELD: 8 servings

Masala Soup

This thick and hearty soup is almost stewlike. It eats like a meal, especially if you throw in some broccoli and carrots!

- 2 tablespoons (30 ml) olive oil
- 1 yellow onion, diced
- 8 cups (2 L) water
- 1 jar Masala Soup Mix

Heat the olive oil in a large soup pot with a tight fitting lid over medium-high heat. Add the diced onion and sauté until translucent and fragrant, 4 to 6 minutes.
Add the water and the contents of the jar. Stir to combine. Bring to a boil over high heat, then reduce the heat to a simmer, cover, and simmer for 45 minutes, or until the split peas and rice are tender. Remove the bay leaf before serving.

Yield: 8 servings

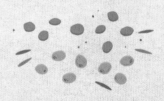

Gift It!

Tie a pretty ribbon or twine around the top of the jar and add the recipe card.

Cheesy Potato Soup Mix

This soup is the perfect introduction of nutritional yeast to those who might normally be, like, "No way am I eating that weird yellow powder you swear has a nutty, cheesy flavor that is full of vitamins, minerals, protein, and fiber!"

3 cups (171 g) instant potato flakes (ingredients should include only potatoes and possibly an anti-caking agent)

½ cup (80 g) nutritional yeast

½ cup (48 g) vegetable broth powder

2 tablespoons (4 g) dried chives

2 teaspoons ground mustard

1 teaspoon sea salt

1 teaspoon onion powder

1 teaspoon garlic powder

¼ teaspoon ground black pepper

¼ teaspoon paprika

¼ teaspoon turmeric

Mix all the ingredients together in a mixing bowl until well combined.

YIELD: 4½ cups (745 g)

Cheesy Potato Soup

To serve 8:
- 6 cups (1.4 L) water
- ½ cup (112 g) nondairy butter
- 3 cups (705 ml) nondairy milk
- 1 jar Cheesy Potato Soup Mix

To serve 4:
- 3 cups (705 ml) water
- ¼ cup (56 g) nondairy butter
- 1 ½ cups (355 ml) nondairy milk
- ½ jar Cheesy Potato Soup Mix

To serve 1:
- 1 cup (235 ml) water
- 1 tablespoon (14 g) nondairy butter
- ½ cup (120 ml) nondairy milk
- ½ cup Cheesy Potato Soup Mix

Add the water and butter to a large soup pot and bring to a boil over medium-high heat. When the butter has melted, stir in the milk and then the soup mix. Stir until smooth. Remove from the heat.

For a thicker soup, add less milk. For a thinner soup, add more milk. For extra goodness, garnish with a spoonful of imitation bacon bits.

Yield: 4½ cups (745 g)

Gift It!

No need to layer this one, so simply package in a jar or clear bag, and tie closed with a ribbon or twine, and attach the recipe card above.

Instant Macaroni and Cheese Mix

This mix is a great gift for busy vegans, new vegans, or any vegan! It also makes a nice item to bring to a bake sale. It's not a cookie or a cupcake, and every time I bring some to bake sales, they always sell out. The mix is also naturally gluten and soy free, so it is an amazing gift for those with food sensitivities.

3 cups (413 g) raw cashews

2 cups (240 g) nutritional yeast

½ cup (64 g) arrowroot powder

3 tablespoons (45 g) garlic powder

3 tablespoons (45 g) onion powder

1 tablespoon (18 g) sea salt

1 tablespoon (8 g) ground mustard seed

2 teaspoons paprika

1 teaspoon dried parsley

1 teaspoon dried green onion

½ teaspoon turmeric

½ teaspoon ground black pepper

¼ teaspoon cayenne pepper (or chili powder for less heat)

¼ teaspoon ground cumin

Using a very dry blender or a coffee grinder, grind the cashews in small batches into a very fine powder. Add to a container with a tight-fitting lid, then add all the remaining ingredients and shake vigorously until well mixed.

YIELD: 5 cups (950 g)

Instant Macaroni and Cheese

Who would have thought vegan mac and cheese could ever be so easy?

- Heaping ½ cup (100 g) Instant Macaroni and Cheese Mix
- 1 cup (235 ml) nondairy milk or water

- 1 pound (454 g) pasta, prepared according to package instructions

Combine the mix and milk in a saucepot over medium heat. Cook, stirring constantly, until thickened. Add to the prepared pasta for instant mac and cheese!

Once the package is opened, store in the refrigerator for up to a month, or freeze indefinitely.

Yield: 4 main dish or 8 side dish servings

Gift It!

Package in mason jars, clear cellophane bags, or any container with a tight-fitting lid. Be sure to tie on the recipe card with a pretty ribbon.

Fruity Curried Rice Pilaf Mix

Why not make up a bunch of these mixes for the next community vegan bake sale? They look real pretty in mason jars, and make a lovely gift as well.

¼ cup (24 g) vegetable broth powder

¼ cup (30 g) dried cranberries

1 cup (180 g) uncooked basmati or jasmine rice

6 dried apricots, diced

¼ cup (27 g) slivered or sliced almonds

1 tablespoon (7 g) turmeric

1 tablespoon (8 g) onion powder

1 teaspoon dried parsley

½ teaspoon coriander

½ teaspoon ground cumin

¼ teaspoon cayenne pepper (adjust heat to taste)

¼ teaspoon ground cardamom

In a 16-ounce (454 g) mason jar, layer the broth powder, cranberries, rice, apricots, and almonds.

In a small bowl, mix together the turmeric, onion powder, parsley, coriander, cumin, cayenne pepper, and cardamom. Place the spice mixture in a small resealable plastic bag and add on top of the almonds before sealing the jar.

YIELD: 4 servings

Fruity Curried Rice Pilaf

Serve this delicious, almost risottolike pilaf alone as a side dish or add in your favorite vegetables and proteins to make a complete meal.

- 3⅔ cups (865 ml) water
- ¼ cup (60 ml) olive oil
- 1 jar Fruity Curried Rice Pilaf Mix
- Salt to taste

Combine the water, oil, and pilaf mix in a pot with a tight-fitting lid. Stir to mix well. Bring to a boil over high heat, reduce the heat to a simmer, cover, and simmer for 20 minutes, stirring every few minutes to prevent the rice from sticking to the bottom of the pot.

Remove the lid and continue to simmer for 5 to 7 more minutes, stirring almost constantly, until the rice is tender and almost all of the liquid has been absorbed.

Add salt to taste.

Yield: 4 servings

Gift It!

Tie on the recipe card to the jar with a pretty ribbon or twine.

TVP Taco Meat Mix

This easy mix makes for a great taco and burrito filler.

1 cup (65 g) TVP granules

2 teaspoons chili powder

1 teaspoon garlic powder

1 teaspoon onion powder

1 teaspoon evaporated cane
   juice or granulated sugar

1 teaspoon ground cumin

1 teaspoon paprika

½ teaspoon cayenne pepper
   or chipotle powder

½ teaspoon salt

Mix all the ingredients together and place in a clear bag or jar and attach the recipe card below.

YIELD: 2½ cups (312 g)

TVP Taco Meat

- 1 jar TVP Taco Meat Mix
- 1 cup (235 ml) boiling water
- 2 tablespoons (30 ml) olive oil or mild-flavored vegetable oil

Combine the mix, boiling water, and olive oil in a heat-safe bowl. Cover and let sit for 10 minutes.

Fluff with a fork and use in tacos, burritos, or anywhere else you'd use a Mexican-spiced "meat."

Yield: 2½ cups (312 g)

To:

From:

Cajun Red Beans and Rice Mix

Mixes like this are not only gifts, but they are also
super nice to have on hand for easy dinners during a busy week.

2 cups (360 g) uncooked white rice

1 tablespoon (1 g) dried parsley

1 tablespoon (2 g) dried chives

2 teaspoons sea salt

1 teaspoon onion powder

1 teaspoon garlic powder

½ teaspoon smoked paprika

½ teaspoon dried basil

½ teaspoon ground black pepper

¼ teaspoon cayenne pepper

¼ teaspoon dried oregano

¼ teaspoon dried thyme

1 bay leaf

1 cup (185 g) dried small red beans

Place the rice in the bottom of a quart-size mason jar.

Mix together the spices and bay leaf, and place in a small resealable plastic bag. Place the seasoning bag on top of the rice in the jar. Top with the red beans and seal.

YIELD: 8 servings

Cajun Red Beans and Rice

Remove the beans from the jar. Remove the seasoning packet and set aside. Rinse the beans under cold running water. Add the beans and 4 cups (1 L) water to a large stockpot or Dutch oven with a tight-fitting lid. Bring to a boil over high heat. Reduce the heat to a simmer and cook, uncovered, for 2 minutes. Remove from the heat, cover, and let stand for 1 hour. Drain and rinse the beans. Return the beans to the pot. Add 8 cups (2 L) fresh water and the seasoning packet. Bring to a boil over high heat, reduce the heat to a simmer, and cook, covered, for 60 minutes, stirring every 20 minutes or so. Add the rice and stir to combine. Simmer, covered, for about 30 minutes, stirring often, until the rice and beans are tender and almost all of the water has been absorbed. Discard the bay leaf before serving.

Yield: 8 servings

Gift It!

Tie on the recipe card to a quart-size jar with a pretty ribbon or twine.

Chipotle Ranch Dressing Mix

Ranch dressing took the top spot as America's favorite dressing in 1992, when it surpassed Italian dressing. In addition to a great salad topper, ranch makes a delicious dipping sauce for veggies and, of course, fried foods.

¼ cup (20 g) panko-style bread crumbs

¼ cup (4 g) dried parsley

1 tablespoon (8 g) onion powder

1 tablespoon (8 g) garlic powder

2 teaspoons dried dillweed

1 ½ teaspoons sea salt

½ teaspoon chipotle powder

½ teaspoon ground cumin

¼ teaspoon ground black pepper

Mix everything together in a bowl.

YIELD: ¾ cup (72 g)

Chipotle Ranch Dressing

This blend tastes great right out of the jar sprinkled on salads and pasta, or even mixed into veggie burgers. When prepared, it makes a great salad dressing or dip for veggies and chips.

For Salad Dressing: Combine 2 tablespoons (12 g) mix with 1 cup (224 g) vegan mayonnaise, ½ cup (120 ml) unsweetened nondairy milk, and 1 tablespoon (15 ml) lemon juice. Store in an airtight container in the refrigerator.

For Dip: Combine 3 tablespoons (18 g) mix with 12 ounces (340 g) nondairy sour cream and 1 tablespoon (15 ml) lemon juice. Store in an airtight container in the refrigerator.

Yield: 1½ cups (340 g) dressing or dip

Fajita and Taco Seasoning Mix

This recipe yields about 3 full cups (525 g) of mix,
which is a lot, so it is perfect for making many gifts at once.

½ cup (64 g) granulated garlic

½ cup (64 g) granulated onion

½ cup (100 g) evaporated cane juice or sugar

½ cup (56 g) smoked paprika

½ cup (64 g) chili powder (I like it hot, but you can adjust according to your taste)

½ cup (144 g) fine sea salt

¼ cup (48 g) ground cumin

2 tablespoons (16 g) chipotle powder

1 tablespoon (8 g) ground black pepper

Mix all the ingredients together until well combined.

YIELD: 3 cups (525 g)

Fajita and Taco Seasoning

Use this tasty seasoning on salads or pasta, sprinkle it over fajita veggies while cooking, use it as a dry rub on tofu, or make delicious fillings for burritos and tacos.

- 2 heaping tablespoons (22 g) Fajita and Taco Seasoning Mix
- 1 cup (96 g) TVP granules or Soy Curls
- 2 tablespoons (30 ml) olive or vegetable oil
- 1 cup (235 ml) boiling water

Stir together the seasoning mix with the TVP or Soy Curls. Stir in the oil and boiling water. Cover and let stand for 10 minutes before using.

Yield: 1½ cups (268 g)

Gift It!

Package these mixes in seasoning shaker jars, in clear bags, or in Super Simple Gift Envelopes (page 12), like the ranch dressing packets from the market, and attach the recipe card above. When I give shaker jars, I always put a layer of plastic wrap over the top of the jar before screwing on the cap, to preserve freshness and prevent spills.

Chapter 4

A Tisket, a Tasket, a Yummy Vegan Basket

Themed Gift Baskets

This chapter is more than how to put together the ultimate foodie gift basket. It's more about how to think outside the basket! Some of the best food gifts aren't even packaged in baskets. Rather, they are put together in meaningful, useful vessels, such as colanders, ice buckets, storage boxes, mixing bowls, and boxes.

But even more important than the vessel is the stuff you put inside it. Anyone can grab a bunch of stuff from the market, put it in a basket, throw a ribbon on it, and call it done. But when you really put some thought into it, and make some, if not most, of the contents from scratch, well, the love shines through and that everyday gift is transformed into something really special.

This chapter is divided into seven sections, each one containing recipes and projects to put together some amazing food-themed gifts. Whether you need to put together a sweet gift for the chocolate lover in your life, a game-day smorgasbord for the football fanatic, or a party pack for girls' margarita night in, I've got you covered.

Chocolate Lover's Gift Basket

Dark, rich, decadent chocolate. We all know someone who absolutely loves the stuff. This is the basket for that special person. Filled with homemade treats, this basket is sure to please.

To make this gift basket, find a basket that has a purpose other than delivering the goods. The one shown here is a picnic basket. Line the bottom of the basket with a pair of fabric napkins or Reversible Hand-Stitched Placemats (page 117). Then it's time to fill it up with chocolate goodness. The recipes for Brownie Bites, Chocolate-Covered Caramel Nut Clusters, Chocolate Chip Cookies, and Black and White Drop Cakes all follow. If you want to add a jar of drink mix (as pictured), I suggest the Instant Hot Cocoa Mix on page 112 or the Instant Mocha Mix on page 83. And don't forget to make enough goodies to treat yourself!

Brownie Bites

You know those little brownie bites you always see in the bakery department of the grocery store, but can never buy because they are almost never, ever vegan? Now you can have them to your heart's content.

1 recipe Fudgy Brownie Mix (page 84), prepared

Prepare brownies according to recipe on page 84. I find that these work best when they are so slightly undercooked—not wet, just a little bit moister.

Remove from the oven and allow to cool completely. Cut into 1-inch (2.5 cm) cubes.

Add the powdered sugar and the evaporated cane juice to separate small bowls. Carefully toss half of the brownie bites in the powdered sugar and half in the evaporated cane juice to coat. Toss the bites one at a time to prevent breakage.

YIELD: 80 brownie bites

Chocolate-Covered Caramel Nut Clusters

These treats are all about the nuts. The recipe here is for big clusters, but feel free to use mini cupcake liners to make lots.

1 cup (200 g) evaporated cane juice or granulated sugar

½ cup (112 g) nondairy butter

¼ cup (60 ml) nondairy milk (almond, soy, or coconut works well here; rice is not recommended)

3 cups (360 g) mixed nuts (I use pecans, walnuts, and cashews, but use whatever you fancy!)

3 tablespoons (24 g) cornstarch mixed with ¼ cup (60 ml) water to make a slurry

1 cup (176 g) vegan chocolate chips

1 ounce (28 g) food-grade paraffin wax, such as Parowax (optional)

Line a standard muffin tin with 12 cupcake papers.

In a saucepot over medium to medium-high heat, melt the sugar, butter, and milk. As soon as it begins to boil, stir in the nuts. Return to a boil for 5 full minutes, stirring often.

Add the cornstarch slurry and cook for 2 more minutes, stirring constantly.

Distribute the caramelized nuts evenly among the papers.

Melt the chocolate and wax (if using) in a double boiler or in a stainless steel bowl set over a pot of water. Drizzle the melted chocolate evenly over each cluster.

Allow to cool completely before removing from the pan.

YIELD: 12 candies

Instant Hot Cocoa Mix

This instant cocoa mix is an awesome way to prove that creamy hot cocoa can be had, even without cow's milk! Package the mix in jars or cellophane bags with a tag attached that reads "Mix 2 heaping tablespoons (13 g) of cocoa mix with 8 ounces (235 ml) boiling water. Top with nondairy whipped topping or vegan marshmallows for an extra special treat.

1 cup (80 g) unsweetened cocoa powder

2 cups (240 g) powdered sugar

1 cup (92 g) powdered rice milk
(soy not recommended)

In a large mixing bowl, stir together all the ingredients until well combined.

YIELD: 4 cups (412 g)

Chocolate Chip Cookies

What respectable chocolate lover's basket would be complete without chocolate chip cookies?

½ cup (112 g) nondairy butter, softened

1 cup (215 g) firmly packed light brown sugar

¾ cup (150 g) evaporated cane juice or granulated sugar

1 ½ teaspoons vanilla extract

¼ cup (60 g) nondairy milk

¼ cup (60 g) maple syrup

¼ cup (60 g) vegetable oil

2 ½ cups (313 g) all-purpose flour

¼ cup (32 g) cornstarch

1 teaspoon baking soda

½ teaspoon salt

1 cup (176 g) vegan chocolate chips

½ teaspoon fine sea salt

Preheat the oven to 375°F (190°C, or gas mark 5). Line 4 baking sheets with parchment or silicone mats.

Using an electric mixer, beat together the butter, brown sugar, evaporated cane juice, vanilla, milk, syrup, and oil.

In a separate bowl, mix together the flour, cornstarch, baking soda, and salt.

Slowly add the flour mixture to the wet ingredients. Fold in the chocolate chips.

From here you can make the cookies immediately, or form the dough into a log, wrap it in plastic, and refrigerate it for later use.

Form about 1 heaping tablespoon (35 g) dough into balls and place on the baking sheets, spacing them 3 inches (7.5 cm) apart. Place no more than 8 per sheet, because they spread a lot. Gently press each ball with the back of a spoon to slightly flatten. Sprinkle the tiniest amount of fine sea salt on each cookie.

Bake for 10 minutes on the center rack, rotating the pan halfway through.

Remove from the oven and allow to cool for 5 minutes before transferring to a wire rack to cool completely.

YIELD: 32 cookies

Black-and-White Drop Cakes

Black-and-white cookies are more like flat little cakes then cookies. A hint of lemon in the batter gives these soft cookies that little something special. I do like to make them HUGE and then wrap them up in plastic wrap, but I find the smaller ones are easier to handle, so the recipe is for a smaller version. If you want to give the big ones a go, use ¼ cup (80 g) batter per cookie. Make these within a day or two of when you plan to gift them, because they don't have a very long shelf life.

For Cookies:

¼ cup (60 g) vegetable oil

1 cup (200 g) evaporated cane juice or granulated sugar

6 ounces (170 g) nondairy yogurt (I use lemon, but plain or vanilla will work, too)

½ cup (120 ml) nondairy milk

1 teaspoon vanilla extract

1 teaspoon lemon extract

2 cups (250 g) all-purpose flour

2 teaspoons baking powder

1 teaspoon baking soda

½ teaspoon salt

For Icing:

2 cups (240 g) powdered sugar

¼ cup (60 g) nondairy milk, divided

2 tablespoons (30 ml) light corn syrup (or agave nectar, but it won't be as white)

¾ cup (132 g) vegan chocolate chips

¼ cup (20 g) cocoa powder

Preheat the oven to 400°F (200°C, or gas mark 6). Line baking sheets with parchment or silicone baking mats.

To make the cookies: Add the oil, evaporated cane juice, yogurt, milk, vanilla, and lemon extract to a mixing bowl and stir to combine.

Add the flour, baking powder, baking soda, and salt to the mixture. Mix until well combined. The batter will be light yet thick and sticky.

Drop 2 heaping tablespoons (40 g) batter onto the prepared baking sheets, spacing them at least 2 inches (5 cm) apart.

Bake for 10 minutes, or until golden. Remove from the oven and allow to cool for 10 minutes before transferring to a wire rack to cool completely.

To make the icing: Mix together the powdered sugar, 2 tablespoons (30 ml) of the nondairy milk, and the corn syrup until smooth.

Flip the completely cooled cookies over and paint half of each cookie's flat side with the "white" icing. You will use about two-thirds of the icing. Return to the cooling rack to harden.

Add the remaining icing to a double boiler (or a stainless steel bowl set over a pot of water) and add the chocolate chips, cocoa, and remaining 2 tablespoons (30 ml) milk. Heat and stir until the chocolate is melted and smooth.

Paint each of the cookie's other half with the "black" icing. Return to the rack to cool and harden completely.

YIELD: 24 cookies (or 12 huge ones!)

Margarita Party Bucket

The classic lime margarita is a party favorite! Unfortunately, so many people rely on that neon green mix full of artificial flavors and colors found at most supermarkets. Show your friends and family what an all-natural margarita tastes like . . . delicious!

The components of this gift are simple and useful. Into an ice bucket pack up a jar of homemade Classic Lime Margarita Mix, Lime Salt, a bottle of tequila, two margarita glasses, and a couple of limes. It's everything you need to guarantee an evening of refreshingly good times.

Classic Lime Margarita Mix

1 cup (200 g) evaporated cane juice or granulated sugar

1 orange, sliced into 8 slices, peel left on

3 ½ cups (823 ml) water

1 cup (235 ml) lime juice

½ cup (120 ml) lemon juice

¼ cup (60 ml) agave nectar

Add the sugar, orange slices, and water to a pot. Bring to a boil over high heat, reduce the heat to a simmer, and simmer for 15 minutes, making sure all of the sugar gets dissolved.

Remove from the heat. Stir in the lime juice, lemon juice, and agave nectar.

Allow to cool completely. Strain and bottle. Attach the recipe card below.

YIELD: 5 cups (1.2 L)

Lime Salt

1 cup (288 g) coarse sea salt

¼ cup (60 ml) lime juice

A few drops natural green food coloring (optional)

Preheat the oven to 150°F (66°C, or your oven's lowest setting). Line a baking sheet with aluminum foil.

Mix the salt with the lime juice and food coloring, if using. Spread in a single layer on the baking sheet.

Bake at for about 1 hour, or until all of the liquid has been absorbed.

Allow to cool completely before packaging.

YIELD: 1 cup (288 g)

Classic Lime Margaritas

- ½ cup (112 g) Classic Lime Margarita Mix
- Lime Salt

- ¼ cup (60 ml) tequila blanco
- Lime wedge (optional)

Rub the rim of the glass with margarita mix and dip in the salt. Add ice, the tequila, and the remaining margarita mix to a cocktail shaker and shake.

Pour into a glass. Garnish with a lime wedge if desired. Keep the mix refrigerated to maintain freshness.

Yield: 1 serving

A Night at the Movies at Home

One of my favorite things to do on a Saturday night is to don my fuzzy slippers, pop up a huge bowl of popcorn, cuddle up on the couch with my husband and the girls, and watch a good classic movie. If someone had given me this gift, I would have given her a big kiss!

To put this gift together, start with a big popcorn bowl to pile in all of the goodies. Line the bowl with two (or more) Reversible Hand-Stitched Placemats (page 117), and then stuff that bowl full of classic movie treats. Be sure to add a bag of un-popped popcorn, paper popcorn bags, Goobernets, Sweet Popcorn Topper, Savory Popcorn Topper, and a classic movie on a DVD.

Reversible Hand-Stitched Placemats

This is a great way to use up scrap fabric. You can add fringe, rickrack, dingle balls, ribbons, buttons, appliqués, ruffles, simple piping, or any kind of accoutrements to these adorable placemats.

Iron

Fabric

Measuring tape

Scissors

Felt interfacing

Pins

Needle with a large eye

Embroidery thread or yarn

Notions, for decorating (optional)

1. Press the fabric to eliminate wrinkles and creases.
2. Measure and cut two rectangles of fabric, each 13 ½ x 19 ¼ inches (34 x 49 cm).
3. Measure and cut one rectangle of felt interfacing to 12 ½ x 18 ½ inches (32 x 47 cm).
4. Fold over a ¼-inch (6 mm) seam allowance and press in place on all four sides of both fabric rectangles.
5. Sandwich the felt interfacing between the two fabric panels. Pin in place.
6. With a needle and embroidery thread, finish the edges using a simple blanket stitch. Add any notions, if desired.
7. Press flat.
8. Repeat to make as many placemats as desired.

Goobernets

Goobers + Raisinets = Goobernets! Two classic movie candies combined.

1 cup (176 g) vegan chocolate chips, white or dark or both

1 ounce (28 g) Parowax (optional)

36 raisins

36 dry-roasted peanuts

Melt the chocolate and wax, if using, in a double boiler. If you don't have a double boiler, just do as I do, and place a stainless steel mixing bowl over a pot of water. Take care not to get water in your melting chocolate.

Add 3 peanuts and 3 raisins to each of 12 mini cupcake liners. Carefully spoon the melted chocolate to cover the nuts and raisins and to fill the cups about three-fourths full.

Allow to cool and harden completely before packaging.

YIELD: 12 candies

Gift It!

Package in a Truffle Gift Box (page 14) or Super Simple Gift Envelope (page 12) and affix a pretty ribbon or twine.

Sweet Popcorn Topper

Adding this chocolaty topper to popcorn makes for an addicting (and low-fat) snack!

¾ cup (150 g) evaporated cane juice or
   granulated sugar

2 tablespoons (10 g) cocoa powder

1 tablespoon (5 g) vanilla powder

1 teaspoon ground cinnamon

½ teaspoon ground nutmeg

Mix the ingredients together until well combined.

YIELD: 1 cup (175 g)

Gift It!

Package these popcorn toppers in separate spice shakers. Attach Hang Tags (pages 30–33) with the recipe title and directions on how to use: "To use, sprinkle a liberal amount all over freshly popped popcorn."

Savory Popcorn Topper

Mushrooms? On popcorn? You bet'cha! And now that you've learned this secret, you'll be doing all kinds of fun things with dried mushroom powder.

1 ounce (28 g) dried shiitake mushrooms, ground into a fine powder

2 tablespoons (20 g) nutritional yeast

2 tablespoons (12 g) vegetable broth powder

1 tablespoon (18 g) sea salt

1 ½ teaspoons garlic powder

1 ½ teaspoons onion powder

1 ½ teaspoons dried parsley

½ teaspoon paprika

½ teaspoon dried dillweed

½ teaspoon dried oregano

½ teaspoon ground black pepper

Mix the ingredients together until well combined.

YIELD: 1 cup (165 g)

Pasta Party

Who doesn't love a nice pasta dinner? A colander lined with a couple of fabric napkins or Reversible Hand-Stitched Placemats (page 117) and stuffed with all the necessary ingredients—pasta; Roasted Garlic; Rosemary-Infused Olive Oil; Italian Spiced Parm-y Sprinkles; Sun-Dried Tomato, Basil, and Garlic Pasta and Pizza Sauce; and a pasta spoon thrown in there for good measure—makes a wonderfully thoughtful gift anyone would be excited to receive.

Roasted Garlic

I always keep at least a jar full of roasted garlic on hand to use for garlic bread or on pasta or steamed vegetables. The process is really simple, and it makes for a very nice gift.

6 heads garlic (about 40 whole cloves), cloves separated and peeled but left whole

2 tablespoons (30 ml) olive oil

¼ teaspoon fine sea salt

Additional olive oil, for topping off

Preheat the oven to 350°F (180°C, or gas mark 4).

Add the garlic, 2 tablespoons (30 ml) olive oil, and salt to the center of a square of aluminum foil. Wrap loosely.

Roast for 30 minutes, then remove from the oven and carefully unwrap the foil.

Carefully transfer the roasted cloves to an 8-ounce (235 ml) jar. Top off with the additional olive oil and seal.

YIELD: 1 (8-ounce, or 235 ml) jar

Gift It!

Tie on a pretty Hang Tag (pages 30–33) or affix a nice Label (pages 30–31).

Rosemary-Infused Olive Oil

This herb-infused oil lends an earthy flavor to whatever you add it to.

1 ½ cups (355 ml) extra-virgin olive oil

3 sprigs fresh rosemary

Add the oil and rosemary to a 12-ounce (355 ml) jar or bottle. Seal. Store in a cool dark place. The longer it sits, the more flavorful it gets.

YIELD: 1 ½ cups (355 ml)

Gift It!

Find a really nice bottle or jar for this, and then tie on a pretty Hang Tag (pages 30–33) or affix a nice Label (pages 30–31).

Italian-Spiced Parm-y Sprinkles

Quick and tasty, this is worth making a double batch—
one for the gift basket and one for yourself.

½ cup (60 g) walnut pieces

½ cup (60 g) nutritional yeast

½ cup (40 g) panko-style bread crumbs

½ teaspoon dried basil

¼ teaspoon fennel seed

¼ teaspoon dried parsley

¼ teaspoon dried oregano

¼ teaspoon dried marjoram

¼ to ½ teaspoon salt, to taste

Add all the ingredients to a blender or food processor and pulse until the walnut pieces have been ground into a powder.

YIELD: About 1 ½ cups (126 g)

Gift It!

Package in a glass shaker jar (place plastic wrap over the jar top before screwing on the shaker top to seal) and tie a Hang Tag (pages 30–33) to the top of the jar with ribbon or twine. Be sure to include the following on the label: "Use these Italian Spiced Parm-y Sprinkles the same way you would use grated Parmesan cheese. Refrigerate after opening to maximize freshness."

Sun-Dried Tomato, Basil, and Garlic Pasta and Pizza Sauce

This sauce is ripe with traditional flavor. Leave it chunky or purée it smooth. Either way, it makes for a great pasta or pizza sauce! For more on canning, see chapter 5.

2 tablespoons (30 ml) extra-virgin olive oil

6 cloves garlic, minced

1 cup (160 g) finely diced white or yellow onion

28 ounces (784 g) canned diced tomatoes with juice, no salt added

16 ounces (454 g) tomato sauce

3 tablespoons (17 g) tomato paste

¼ cup (28 g) chopped sun-dried tomatoes

¼ cup (60 ml) lemon juice

1 tablespoon (2 g) dried basil, or 3 tablespoons (9 g) fresh, chopped

1 teaspoon dried oregano

½ teaspoon fennel seed

½ teaspoon sea salt

¼ teaspoon ground black pepper

1 tablespoon (13 g) sugar

1 tablespoon (15 ml) maple syrup

For Canning:

4 (16-ounce, or 470 ml) jars

Other "Materials Needed," page 137

In the bottom of a stockpot, heat the olive oil over medium heat. Add the garlic and onion and sauté until the garlic is fragrant and the onions are translucent, about 10 minutes.

Add the tomatoes, tomato sauce, tomato paste, sun-dried tomatoes, lemon juice, basil, oregano, fennel, salt, pepper, sugar, and maple syrup to the pot. Bring to a simmer over medium-low heat. Cover and continue to simmer for 20 more minutes.

Uncover and simmer for 10 more minutes. At this point, decide whether you want chunky pasta sauce or a smooth sauce more suitable for pizza. If chunky is preferred, proceed to canning. If smooth is preferred, use an immersion blender (or very carefully transfer to a blender) to blend until smooth.

Follow canning instructions as outlined in "Canning Basics" on pages 136–139. Processing time is 15 minutes. Any jars that did not seal need to be stored in the refrigerator and used within a week. Refrigerate after opening.

YIELD: 4 (16-ounce, 470 ml) jars

Gift It!

Don't forget to add a handwritten Label (pages 30–31) or a Hang Tag (pages 30–33) to let everyone know this gift was made with love!

It's Game Time!

Throw some microbrews, Bar Nuts, Spicy Nacho Popcorn Topper, and Tofu Jerky into an ice bucket stuffed with a couple of bright green sweat towels (because watching the big game on TV is hard work!), and you've got the perfect gift for the sports lover in your life.

Bar Nuts

These nuts are so addictive! It's a good thing the batch is big, because you'll be snacking on them while putting together the rest of the gift basket. If you don't have any maple syrup on hand, use agave nectar or corn syrup.

½ cup (120 ml) olive oil

¼ cup (60 ml) maple syrup

1 tablespoon (2 g) dried parsley

½ teaspoon dried sage

½ teaspoon dried rosemary

½ teaspoon dried thyme

¼ teaspoon cayenne pepper

1 cup (112 g) cashews

1 cup (140 g) almonds

1 cup (133 g) Brazil nuts

1 cup (99 g) pecans

1 cup (120 g) walnuts

½ teaspoon salt

¼ teaspoon black pepper

Preheat the oven to 350°F (180°C, or gas mark 4). Line a baking sheet with aluminum foil.

In a small bowl, mix together the oil, maple syrup, parsley, sage, rosemary, thyme, and cayenne pepper.

In a separate large mixing bowl, combine all of the nuts. Add the spice mixture and toss to coat completely. Arrange in a single layer on the prepared baking sheet. Rinse and dry the mixing bowl.

Bake for 30 minutes, turning the nuts every 7 or 8 minutes, being careful not to burn.

Remove from the oven and return to the mixing bowl. Add the salt and pepper and toss to coat. Let cool.

Package in an airtight container or sealed bag. Store in a cool, dry place for up to two weeks.

YIELD: 5 cups (600 g)

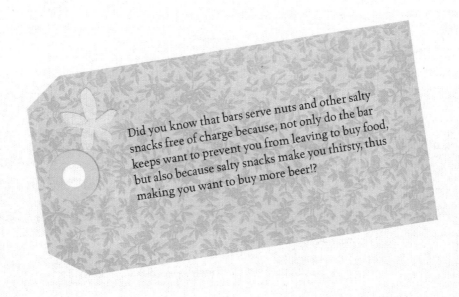

Did you know that bars serve nuts and other salty snacks free of charge because, not only do the bar keeps want to prevent you from leaving to buy food, but also because salty snacks make you thirsty, thus making you want to buy more beer!?

Spicy Nacho Popcorn Topper

This mix makes it possible for vegans to enjoy cheese popcorn again!
Vegan or not, this blend is awesome. You can package this spice blend in a jar to
add to the bucket, but if your sports fan is anything like mine, you'll probably
want to pop up a batch of popcorn and do the mixing for him!

½ cup (80 g) nutritional yeast

1 tablespoon (8 g) garlic powder

1 tablespoon (18 g) sea salt

1 tablespoon (13 g) evaporated cane juice
   or granulated sugar

1 tablespoon (8 g) onion powder

1 tablespoon (2 g) dried chives

1 teaspoon ground cumin

½ teaspoon chipotle powder

½ teaspoon ground black pepper

½ teaspoon red pepper flakes

Mix all the ingredients together until well combined.

YIELD: 1 cup (160 g)

Gift It!

Package in a spice shaker. Attach a Hang Tag (pages 30–33) with the recipe title and these directions: "To use, sprinkle a liberal amount over freshly popped popcorn."

Tofu Jerky

This jerky makes a great gift for outdoorsy vegans and also for the boys. Sometimes homemade gifts tend to have a bit of a feminine quality to them, so it's nice to have an option or two for the fellas. Even though this recipe is part of the larger gift basket, meant for the sports lover on your gift list, the jerky makes a great gift all on its own.

2 pounds (908 g) extra- or super-firm tofu (I like Wildwood Super Firm)

¼ cup (60 ml) soy sauce or tamari

3 tablespoons (45 ml) liquid smoke

½ cup (120 ml) maple syrup

¼ cup (60 ml) vegan Worcestershire sauce

2 tablespoons (12 g) coarsely ground black pepper

Press the excess moisture from the tofu by sandwiching it between paper towels or clean kitchen towels and placing a heavy book or pot on top. Allow to sit for 1 hour.

Slice the tofu into thin, jerky-size slices, about ⅛ inch (3 mm) thick. I usually slice my block in half through the center first and then cut it into strips.

In a mixing bowl, whisk together the soy sauce, liquid smoke, maple syrup, Worcestershire, and pepper. Add the tofu slices, cover with plastic wrap, and marinate overnight in the refrigerator.

Preheat the oven to 200°F (93°C, or gas mark ¼). Line two baking sheets with parchment.

Arrange the tofu in a single layer on the prepared baking sheets.

Bake anywhere from 4 to 8 hours, depending on the moisture content and thickness of your tofu. Flip the pieces once every hour.

Alternatively, you can use a food dehydrator, following the instructions on your machine.

The tofu is done when both sides are the same color— dark chocolate brown—and the pieces are stiff, not floppy. There should be a bit of moisture left in the jerky, but it should be dry to the touch.

YIELD: About 48 pieces

Gift It!

If you have a food saver–type vacuum sealer, it's a perfect way to package this. If not, you can just pack it in resealable plastic bags or stuff a whole bunch into a big mason jar. Attach a custom Label (pages 30–31).

Is It Delivery? Nope, Even Better! It's Homemade!

One of my very first culinary adventures as a grown-up in my own apartment was to make homemade pizza for my friends. I felt so cool. So accomplished. And I have been making pizza at home ever since. Providing the tools and ingredients necessary to turn any kitchen into a pizzeria is a great host or hostess gift.

To put together this gift, all you need is a big mixing bowl. Line it with a couple of fabric napkins, and then add Pizza Topper Spice Blend; TVP Pepperoni Mix; Sun-Dried Tomato, Basil, and Garlic Pasta and Pizza Sauce (page 123); and Homemade Pizza Dough Mix. Finish it off with a couple of pizza plates and a rotary pizza cutter.

Homemade Pizza Dough Mix

By gathering all the ingredients to make pizza dough at home, there's no reason to resort to the cardboardlike stuff they try to pass off as pizza crust at the market.

2 cups (250 g) all-purpose flour

½ cup (72 g) vital wheat gluten flour

½ teaspoon salt

1 (¼-ounce, or 7 g) packet active dry yeast

1 teaspoon sugar

Combine the flours and salt in a bowl and stir well. Pour in to a bag or jar. Place the yeast packet and sugar in a small plastic bag, and place on top of the flour. Attach the recipe card below.

YIELD: 2 pizzas

Pizza as You Please

- 1 jar Homemade Pizza Dough Mix
- 1 cup (235 ml) warm water, divided
- 1 tablespoon (15 ml) olive oil, plus more for brushing
- Toppings of your choice

Remove the yeast packet and sugar from the mix and add to a bowl. Add ½ cup (120 ml) of the warm water and let stand for 10 minutes. Pour the flour mixture into a mixing bowl. Add the yeast mixture, remaining ½ cup (120 ml) water, and 1 tablespoon (15 ml) olive oil. Knead for about 10 minutes. Divide the dough in half and form each into a ball. Brush with a light coat of olive oil, cover the bowl with plastic wrap, and let rise for 1 hour. Preheat the oven to 450°F (230°C, or gas mark 8). Line 2 baking sheets with parchment. Punch down each dough ball and knead for 2 to 3 minutes. On a lightly floured surface, roll out each dough ball into a pizza crust of your desired thickness. Transfer to the baking sheets. Add your favorite toppings and bake for 10 minutes, or until the crust is a nice golden brown.

Yield: 2 pizzas

TVP Pepperoni Mix

Pepperoni need not be a thing of the past for vegans. This spicy mix tastes just like the real thing when sprinkled over homemade pizza.

1 cup (96 g) TVP granules

1 tablespoon (7 g) paprika

1 tablespoon (8 g) garlic powder

1 teaspoon ground black pepper

1 teaspoon aniseed

1 teaspoon sea salt

1 teaspoon red pepper flakes

1 teaspoon sugar

1 teaspoon dried basil

1 teaspoon cayenne pepper or chipotle powder

Combine all the ingredients and package in a jar or bag with the recipe card below.

YIELD: 1¼ cups (250 g)

TVP Pepperoni

- 1 jar TVP Pepperoni Mix
- 1 cup (235 ml) boiling water
- 2 tablespoons (30 ml) olive oil
- 2 tablespoons (30 ml) liquid smoke
- Toppings of your choice

Combine the mix, boiling water, olive oil, and liquid smoke in a heat-safe bowl.

Cover and let sit for 10 minutes.

Fluff with a fork and use to top a pizza, stuff a calzone, or anywhere else you'd use ground pepperoni!

Yield: 2 cups (470 g)

Gift It!

Package in clear bags and add a handwritten Label (pages 30–31) or tie on a Hang Tag (pages 30–33) noting what the flavor is inside.

Pizza Topper Spice Blend

This spice blend tastes great sprinkled over homemade OR store-bought pizza! It also tastes yummy on pasta and salads, and is especially good on garlic bread.

½ cup (80 g) nutritional yeast

1 tablespoon (7 g) sweet paprika

1 tablespoon (8 g) garlic powder

1 tablespoon (18 g) sea salt

1 tablespoon (8 g) dehydrated minced onion

1 tablespoon (1 g) dried parsley

1 tablespoon (2 g) dried basil

1 teaspoon ground black pepper

1 teaspoon dried oregano

½ teaspoon red pepper flakes

Mix all the ingredients together.

YIELD: About 1 cup (165 g)

Gift It!

Package in a spice shaker. Attach a Hang Tag (page 30–33) with the recipe title and these directions: "To use, sprinkle a liberal amount over pizza, pasta, salads, or garlic bread."

Taco Tuesdays

Restaurants and households around the world celebrate the weekly holiday known as Taco Tuesday. Inspire someone you know to start his or her own Taco Tuesday with this fiesta in a bowl.

Make a big bag of tortilla chips and a jar of Salsa Roja, and add a package of TVP Taco Meat Mix (page 103) and a jar of Fajita and Taco Seasoning Mix (page 107) to a festive chip bowl and you're all set!

Tortilla Chips

Frying up a big batch of tortilla chips makes for a snack that is so much tastier than store-bought chips. I love to make my own flavored chips by liberally sprinkling the chips as they come out of the oil with any of the spice blends in this book.

Corn tortillas

Vegetable oil, for frying

Salt or desired seasoning

Cut the tortillas into triangles.

Fill a deep fryer or a deep pot with 2 inches (5 cm) of vegetable oil and heat the oil to 350°F (180°C). Line a large plate or tray with paper towels or a clean kitchen towel.

Carefully add 8 to 10 tortilla triangles at a time to the hot oil using long-handled tongs. Toss around in the oil for about 1 minute, until golden and crispy. Transfer to the paper towels to drain. Transfer to a large bowl and sprinkle liberally with the salt or seasoning of choice. Return the oil to temperature and repeat with the remaining tortillas.

Allow to cool completely before packaging.

Salsa Roja

This type of salsa is the polar opposite of a chunky salsa fresca or pico de gallo. It has a lot of the same ingredients, but the process is totally different. It's oven-roasted, then puréed. Choose your peppers based on how spicy you like your salsa. For more on canning, see chapter 5.

10 Roma tomatoes, cut in half

8 to 10 cloves garlic, peeled

1 medium white or yellow onion, roughly chopped

6 poblanos (anchos or pasillas) or Anaheim chiles (mild), jalapeño peppers (medium-spicy), or chiles de arbol (*muy caliente!*), stemmed, seeded if desired

Salt and pepper to taste

1 cup (13 g) fresh cilantro leaves

¼ cup (60 ml) lime or lemon juice

2 tablespoons (30 ml) white vinegar

Preheat the oven to 350°F (180°C, or gas mark 4). Line a baking sheet with parchment or a silicone baking mat.

Arrange the tomatoes (cut side up), garlic, onion, and peppers in a single layer on the prepared baking sheet. Sprinkle with salt and pepper.

Bake for 60 minutes, or until soft and beginning to brown around the edges, tossing half way through.

Remove from the oven and carefully transfer to a food processor or blender. (You can also place in a bowl and use an immersion blender.) Add the cilantro, lemon juice, vinegar, and salt and pepper to taste and purée until smooth.

Follow canning instructions as outlined in "Canning Basics," pages 136–139. Processing time is 20 minutes. Any jars that did not seal need to be stored in the refrigerator and used within a week. Refrigerate after opening.

YIELD: 5 (8-ounce, or 235 ml) jars

Sweet Whiskey
Barbecue Sauce!

orange
basil
marmalade

Chapter 5

Jars Full of Goodness

Jams, Jellies, Sauces, and Other Yummy Stuff in Jars

Jams, jellies, sauces, infused oils, and all sorts of deliciousness, all neatly packaged in cutely labeled jars. Perfect for gifting or for a little something different at the next vegan bake sale. No experience canning? That's okay. Step-by-step instructions are included here to help get you past your fears. As soon as you see how easy it is, you'll be canning everything!

Canning Basics

My mom, Kim, moved from the big city out to the country a few years back. When she did, she and her husband, Scott, planted a big organic garden on their land. Tomatoes, peppers, and other yummy veggies and fruits were abundant, and even with the big appetites in our family, there was just too much for us all to use before it went bad. So, she decided to start preserving her bounty. For real! My mom, the retired corporate executive, was now canning her own jams, jellies, salsas, and sauces. I was flabbergasted and super excited at the same time.

Momma was kind enough to open up her country kitchen to me and Celine for a few days that we lovingly came to refer to as Jam-Bonanza. We boiled, filled, and tested many jars full of goodness, and we learned from Momma the safe and proper way to use a boiling water bath canning system at home. Up until then, I was under the impression that this process was complicated and very involved, and relied on a whole bunch of expensive specialized equipment. Here's what I learned: Don't be afraid of the process! It is really not that scary at all, and in the long run, making your own preserves, jams, jellies, sauces, and other delicious jars of goodness will save you tons of money. Besides, they make great gifts!

In this book I will only provide recipes that use a hot water bath or a simple cool to seal canning method. There are pressure cooker canners, but I am not going to go there. I want to keep it simple, affordable, and approachable for the average crafty home cook.

Home canning can be broken down into three basic steps, also known as the three "P"s:

1. Prepare. As my husband often tells me, "Prepare, or prepare to fail!" Make sure you always have your jars, lids, and rings clean and sterilized. Running the jars through a cycle in your dishwasher should suffice. If you don't have a dishwasher, wash your jars in hot, soapy water. While you are preparing your recipe, add your jars, lids, and rings to a pot of hot, not boiling, water until you are ready to use them.

2. Pick. Pick out your recipe and follow it to a "T." There are a lot of factors that can affect the safety of your preserved goods, and I do not want any of you guys (or the people you give your gifts to!) to get sick, so please stick to tried-and-true recipes.

3. Preserve. Preserve your recipe in a hot water bath.

That's it! I feel like we should be reading *There's a Monster at the End of This Book*. (Spoiler alert! There is no monster at the end of the book.)

Believe it or not, most hardware stores carry home canning equipment. I usually buy my jars and lids at the local supermarket. I also found all of my utensils, pectin, and most things I've ever needed at the supermarket. Also, everything can be found on Amazon.com.

Higher altitudes will affect your canning projects, so if you live in a higher altitude, increase the processing time according to the chart below:

Altitude Above Sea Level	Increase Processing Time
1,000 to 3,000 feet (300 to 900 m)	5 minutes
3,000 to 6,000 feet (900 to 1,800 m)	10 minutes
6,000 to 8,000 feet (1,800 to 2,400 m)	15 minutes
8,000 to 10,000 feet (2,400 to 3,000 m)	20 minutes

To read further information on home preserving and canning, the fine folks over at Ball have a great free downloadable PDF on their website (http://freshpreserving.com/guides/IntroToCanning.pdf) with some detailed information laid out in an easy-to-follow format. And, I highly recommend the book *Put 'em Up! A Comprehensive Home Preserving Guide for the Creative Cook, from Drying and Freezing to Canning and Pickling* by Sherri Brooks Vinton. Although it isn't necessarily a vegan book, it is packed full of information on all sorts of home preserving methods. Not to mention that it is cute as a button and laid out in a very accessible format.

Materials Needed:

→ **Jars and lids with rings**

→ **Wide-mouth funnel**

→ **Canning pot, at least 12-quart (11 L) capacity**

→ **Canning rack to fit bottom of canning pot**

→ **Canning tongs**

→ **Magnetic lid lifter, to lift lids and rings from hot water bath**

Don't be Afraid of the Process!

Follow these simple steps to create delicious, homemade jams, jellies, sauces, and more.

Place clean jars, lids, and rings in hot, not boiling, water until ready to fill.

Prepare your recipe.   Remove hot jars and drain.   Ladle recipe into jars using a wide-mouth funnel.

Remove the lids and ring and apply so that it is finger tight. Do not overtighten the rings, because air needs to escape from the jars during the processing.

Carefully lower the jars into the boiling water bath using the canning rack or canning tongs. Process according to time listed in recipe.

Carefully remove the jars from the water bath using canning tongs.

Place the jars in a safe place, where they will remain undisturbed, to cool. Once completely cooled, remove rings and dry any excess moisture. Replace rings.

Classic Strawberry Jam

This classic strawberry jam recipe calls for frozen berries
so that you can make jam all year-round.

For Jam:

5 cups (1 kg) frozen strawberries

1 (1 ¾-ounce, or 49 g) box pectin

½ teaspoon nondairy butter, to
    reduce foaming

5 cups (1 kg) sugar

Zest of 1 lemon

For Canning:

6 to 8 (8-ounce, or 235 ml) jars

6 to 8 rings and lids

Other "Materials Needed," page 137

Thaw and drain the frozen strawberries by placing them in a colander or strainer over a bowl in the refrigerator overnight.

Add the thawed strawberries, pectin, and butter to a saucepot. Bring to a full boil over high heat, stirring constantly and mashing as necessary with a spoon as they cook. There should be plenty of fruit bits.

Add the sugar, and lemon zest. Return to full boil, and boil for 1 full minute, stirring constantly.

Follow canning instructions as outlined in "Canning Basics," on pages 136–139. Processing time is 15 minutes. Any jars that did not seal need to be stored in the refrigerator and used within a week. Refrigerate after opening.

YIELD: 6 to 8 (8-ounce, or 235 ml) jars

Gift It!

One of my favorite ways to package homemade jams is to cut a circle of calico, or any other fabric, with pinking shears to measure about an inch (2.5 cm) larger than the lid and then tie it on with a pretty ribbon, yarn, or twine.

Orange Basil Marmalade

True marmalade is bitter and doesn't require any pectin, because the peel of the orange, which makes it bitter, is also full of natural pectin. That's why this recipe leaves in all of the peel and adds no pectin. It tastes delicious spread on toast, crackers, or a bagel. It also makes a great glaze for seitan, tofu, or tempeh. This recipe makes eight 8-ounce (235 ml) jars of marmalade. If you'd like to make more or less, adjust the amounts accordingly.

For Marmalade:

8 medium-size navel oranges

4 cups (800 g) evaporated cane juice or granulated sugar

2 cups (470 ml) water

24 large fresh basil leaves, cut into a super-fine chiffonade

1 tablespoon (15 ml) vanilla extract

For Canning:

8 (8-ounce, or 235 ml) jars

8 rings and lids

Other "Materials Needed," page 137

Cut the top and bottom off of each orange. Slice each orange into 8 segments and remove the seeds and center pith. Place in a food processor and pulse until the mixture has very tiny bits of peel.

Add the orange purée, sugar, and water to a saucepot. Bring to a boil over high heat, reduce the heat to a simmer, and cook, uncovered, for 20 minutes, stirring often.

Remove from the heat and stir in the basil and vanilla.

Follow canning instructions as outlined in "Canning Basics" on pages 136–139. Processing time is 15 minutes. Any jars that did not seal need to be stored in the refrigerator and used within a week. Refrigerate after opening.

YIELD: 8 (8-ounce, or 235 ml) jars

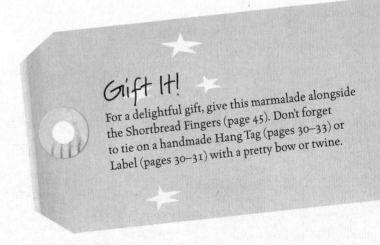

Gift It!

For a delightful gift, give this marmalade alongside the Shortbread Fingers (page 45). Don't forget to tie on a handmade Hang Tag (pages 30–33) or Label (pages 30–31) with a pretty bow or twine.

Lemon Lavender
Curd

handmade with
love!

Lemon Lavender Curd

This recipe makes enough for three 8-ounce (235 ml) jars.
I don't recommend making a double batch at one time because it can be
a bit difficult to handle if using more than what is listed here.

2 cups (400 g) sugar

1 cup (235 ml) lemon juice

Zest of 2 lemons

½ cup (112 g) nondairy butter, cubed

1 tablespoon (3 g) food-grade dried lavender flowers

½ cup (64 g) cornstarch mixed with ¾ cup (180 ml) water to make a slurry

For Canning:

3 (8-ounce, or 235 ml) jars

3 rings and lids

Other "Materials Needed," page 137

Add the sugar and lemon juice to a pot and heat over medium-high heat until just beginning to boil, stirring constantly. As soon as it begins to bubble, reduce the heat to medium. Stir in the lemon zest, then add the butter and stir until melted. Stir in the lavender.

Slowly stir in the cornstarch slurry and continue to stir and cook until thickened. It will happen slowly at first and then all of a sudden it will be very thick. You will know it is the right consistency when the lavender stays suspended in the mixture.

Follow canning instructions as outlined in "Canning Basics" on pages 136–139. Processing time is 15 minutes. Any jars that did not seal need to be stored in the refrigerator and used within a week. Refrigerate after opening.

YIELD: 3 (8-ounce, or 235 ml) jars

Gift It!

Don't forget to tie on a Hang Tag (pages 30–33) or Label (pages 30-31) with a pretty ribbon or twine.

Mango Chutney

Mango chutney is a versatile little bugger. Spread on toast, used in a sandwich, mixed with rice, drizzled on your favorite proteins, or mixed into tofu salad, this condiment can do a lot! Don't be intimidated by the long list of ingredients. It's stuff you most likely have in your pantry, and the recipe is actually a breeze to throw together!

24 ounces (672 g) fresh or frozen mango chunks

1 cup (160 g) diced white onion

1 cup (160 g) diced bell pepper (any color!)

1 cup (220 g) firmly packed brown sugar

1 cup (144 g) currants or raisins

1 cup (235 ml) apple juice

½ cup (120 ml) apple cider vinegar

2 tablespoons (2 g) finely chopped fresh mint

2 tablespoons (30 g) minced garlic

1 teaspoon turmeric

1 teaspoon ground cumin

1 teaspoon sea salt

½ teaspoon red pepper flakes

½ teaspoon cayenne pepper

½ teaspoon ground cinnamon

½ teaspoon ground ginger

For Canning:

4 (8-ounce, or 235 ml) jars

Other "Materials Needed," page 137

Throw all the ingredients into a pot, give it a good stir, and bring to a boil over high heat.

Reduce the heat to a simmer, cover, and let simmer for 20 to 30 minutes, or until the fruit is nice and mushy. If you need to use a hand masher to help it along, feel free.

Follow canning instructions as outlined in "Canning Basics" on pages 136–139. Processing time is 20 minutes. Any jars that did not seal need to be stored in the refrigerator and used within a week. Refrigerate after opening.

YIELD: 4 (8-ounce, or 235 ml) jars

Gift It!

Don't forget to tie on a hand-written Hang Tag (pages 30–33) with a pretty ribbon or twine.

Jalapeño Jam

Growing up, I would always say, "Gross! Who on Earth would want to eat jalapeño jelly?" I know there are many who still have this opinion (my husband included), but as I have grown up, and my taste buds have matured, I simply can't get enough of the stuff. The main problem, however, is that most jalapeño jellies are a very unnatural hue of neon green, so I now make my own, leaving it chunky with pieces of jalapeño in it, which makes it more of a jam than a jelly.

12 whole fresh jalapeños

2 cups (470 ml) apple juice

½ cup (120 ml) apple cider vinegar

1 (1 ¾-ounce, or 49 g) box pectin

½ teaspoon nondairy butter, to reduce foaming

4 cups (800 g) evaporated cane juice or granulated sugar

For Canning:

6 (8-ounce, or 235 ml) jars

6 rings and lids

Other "Materials Needed," page 137

Remove the stems from the jalapeños. If you like it spicy, leave in all the seeds and the cores. Leave some in for a medium-spicy jam, or remove all the seeds and cores for a milder jam.

Using a food processor, chop the jalapeños into a pulp. Add the jalapeño pulp, juice, vinegar, pectin, and butter to a pot. Bring to a boil over high heat, stirring constantly.

Once the mixture comes to a full rolling boil, stir in the sugar. Return to a boil, and boil hard for 1 full minute.

Follow canning instructions as outlined in "Canning Basics" on pages 136–139. Processing time is 20 minutes. Any jars that did not seal need to be stored in the refrigerator and used within a week. Refrigerate after opening.

YIELD: 6 (8-ounce, or 235 ml) jars

Sun-Dried
Tomato,
Garlic, and
Basil Olive
Oil

Infused Olive Oils

Flavored oils are great over pasta and for dipping fresh bread,
sautéing veggies, and drizzling over salads. I love them and could make
a hundred different varieties. But, I will limit myself to just
these two . . . and the one in the Pasta Party gift basket on page 120.

Roasted Garlic and Peppercorn Olive Oil

3 heads (about 24 cloves) garlic, peeled

1 tablespoon (6 g) black peppercorns

Pinch of sea salt

¾ cup (180 ml) extra-virgin olive oil, divided

Preheat the oven to 350°F (180°C, or gas mark 4).

Add the garlic, peppercorns, salt, and 1 tablespoon (15 ml) of the olive oil to the center of a square of aluminum foil. Wrap loosely and roast for 30 minutes.

Carefully transfer the roasted cloves and peppercorns to an 8-ounce (235 ml) jar or bottle and pour in the remaining olive oil to top it off; seal.

Store in a cool dark place. The longer the oil sits, the more flavorful it gets. Use within 2 months.

YIELD: 8 ounces (235 ml)

Sun-Dried Tomato, Garlic, and Basil Olive Oil

6 tablespoons (1 ½ ounces, or 48 g) julienne-cut sun-dried tomatoes

1 head (about 8 cloves) garlic, peeled

1 tablespoon (2 g) dried basil

1 ¼ cups (295 ml) extra-virgin olive oil

Add all the ingredients to a 12-ounce (355 ml) jar or bottle. Seal. Store in a cool dark place. The longer the oil sits, the more flavor it gets. Use within 2 months.

YIELD: 12 ounces (355 ml)

Gift It!

Find some really nice bottles for these, and then tie on a pretty Hang Tags (pages 30–33) or affix a nice Label (pages 30–31) to the face of the bottle or jar.

SoCal Salsa Fresca

This fresh salsa screams with California sunshine.

2 cups (330 g) diced fresh mango

1 cup (13 g) finely diced cilantro

1 cup (160 g) finely diced red onion

1 tablespoon (15 g) minced garlic

1 teaspoon salt

½ teaspoon black pepper

2 jalapeño or serrano chiles, seeded, deveined, and finely diced

¼ cup (60 ml) lime juice

2 tablespoons (30 ml) white vinegar

For Canning:

4 (8-ounce, or 235 ml) jars

4 rings and lids

Other "Materials Needed," page 137

Place all the ingredients in a bowl and stir to combine.

Follow canning instructions as outlined in "Canning Basics" on pages 136–139. Processing time is 15 minutes. Any jars that did not seal need to be stored in the refrigerator and used within a week. Refrigerate after opening.

YIELD: 4 (8-ounce, or 235 ml) jars

Gift It!

Give this salsa along with a bag of homemade Tortilla Chips (page 133) for an extra-special gift. Don't forget to add a handwritten Hand Tag (pages 30–33)!

Spicy Garlic Dill Pickles

This recipe is so simple, you'll have your pickles all jarred up in about the time it takes to boil the water and slice the cucumbers. I wrote this recipe so that you could make one jar or ten! A quick note about fermenting pickles: These pickles are made with a saltwater brine, so they are sometimes referred to as fermented or brined pickles, and they contain lactic acid produced by bacterial fermentation. This process produces a type of pickle known as "refrigerator dills" and are fermented for about one week. During curing, colors and flavors change and acidity increases. They do not require a boiling water bath because of the salt solution, which in this recipe is 7.2 percent, and because they are refrigerated. The recipe below is for one 16-ounce (470 ml) jar. Adjust the amounts to make as many jars as you wish.

For Brine:

For each 1 cup (235 ml) water, use 1 tablespoon (18 g) fine sea salt

For Pickles:

1 tablespoon (6 g) black peppercorns

1 teaspoon whole mustard seed

1 to 2 cucumbers, cut into desired shapes to fit jar

4 cloves garlic, cut in half

1 bay leaf, broken into pieces

1 tablespoon (3 g) fresh dill

1 teaspoon red pepper flakes (adjust according to heat preference; this measure makes for a very spicy pickle!)

For Canning:

1 (16-ounce, or 470 ml) jar, plus ring and lid

To make the brine: Bring the water and salt to boil in a saucepot over high heat. Boil until all the salt is dissolved. Reduce the heat to low and keep warm until ready to pour.

To make the pickles: In a very dry skillet, lightly toast the peppercorns and mustard seed over medium-low heat. Set aside.

Pack the cucumbers into the sterilized jar. Add the garlic, bay leaf, dill, red pepper flakes, toasted peppercorns, and mustard seed to the jar. Pour in the hot brine to fill the jars, allowing ½ inch (1.3 cm) of space at the top.

Place the lid and ring on the jar and give it a good shake to distribute all of the ingredients. Place upright and allow to cool. The lid should self-seal as the brine cools, creating a vacuum in the jar.

Place in a cool dark place for one week, then refrigerate.

YIELD: 1 (16-ounce, or 470 ml) jar

Gift It!

Attach a handwritten Label (pages 30–31) or tie on a Hang Tags (pages 30–33) with a piece of twine. Make sure it's known that these are special homemade pickles that you prepared with love! Also make a note to keep refrigerated.

153

California Chow-Chow

Chow-chow is pickled relish made from a combination of vegetables. Growing up, my family always loved Pennsylvania chow-chow, which was a bit sweeter than its traditional Southern brothers. Well, this is California chow-chow, a bit spicier, a tad sharper, and made with a California mix of cauliflower, carrots, and broccoli. More traditional versions include green beans, asparagus, tomatoes, and onions; feel free to add those if you choose. The recipe below is for one 16-ounce (470 ml) jar. Adjust the amounts to make as many jars as you wish. And just like the pickles (page 153), it uses a 7.2 percent salt brine and requires refrigeration after 1 week of fermentation.

For Brine:

For each 1 cup (235 ml) water, use 1 tablespoon (18 g) fine sea salt

For Chow-Chow:

1 tablespoon (6 g) black peppercorns

1 teaspoon whole mustard seed

1 teaspoon coriander seed

6 broccoli florets

6 cauliflower florets

24 carrot coins

2 cloves garlic, cut in half

1 tablespoon (7 g) chopped sun-dried tomatoes

1 bay leaf, broken into pieces

1 teaspoon fresh dill

1/2 teaspoon dried parsley

1/2 teaspoon dried chives

1/8 teaspoon red pepper flakes

For Canning:

1 (16-ounce, or 470 ml) jar, plus ring and lid

To make the brine: Bring the water and salt to boil in a saucepot over high heat. Boil until all the salt is dissolved. Reduce the heat to low and keep warm until ready to pour.

To make the chow-chow: In a very dry skillet, lightly toast the peppercorns, mustard seed, and coriander seed over medium-low heat. Set aside.

Pack the broccoli, cauliflower, and carrots into the sterilized jar. Add the garlic, sun-dried tomatoes, bay leaf, dill, parsley, chives, red pepper flakes, and toasted spices to the jar. Pour in the hot brine to fill the jar, allowing 1/2 inch (1.3 cm) of space at the top.

Place the lid and ring on the jar and give it a good shake to distribute all of the ingredients.

Place upright and allow to cool. The lid should self-seal as the brine cools, creating a vacuum in the jar. Place in a cool dark place for 1 week, then refrigerate.

YIELD: 1 (16-ounce, or 470 ml) jar

Gift It!

Attach a handwritten Label (pages 30–31) or tie on a Hang Tag (pages 30–33) with a piece of twine. Make sure it's known that this is special homemade chow-chow that you prepared with love! Also make a note to keep refrigerated.

Spinach Artichoke Walnut Pesto

The addition of artichokes to this pesto makes for a creaminess
that is an unexpected and delicious surprise!

10 cups (8 ounces, or 224 g) baby spinach

25 leaves fresh basil

2 cups (470 ml) olive oil

1 cup (120 g) walnuts

8 cloves garlic

4 sun-dried tomatoes

1 (14-ounce, or 400 g) can artichoke
hearts, drained

¼ cup (40 g) nutritional yeast

1 tablespoon (15 ml) lemon juice

1 teaspoon ground black pepper

½ teaspoon sea salt

For Canning:

3 (12-ounce, or 355 ml) jars

3 rings and lids

Other "Materials Needed," page 137

Add all the ingredients to a blender and purée until smooth. You
may need to add the spinach in several batches.

Follow canning instructions as outlined in "Canning Basics"
on pages 136–139. Processing time is 15 minutes. Any jars that
did not seal need to be stored in the refrigerator and used within
a week. Refrigerate after opening.

YIELD: 3 (12-ounce, or 355 ml) jars

Gift It!

Tie a circle of fabric over the
lid with a ribbon or twine
and attach a pretty Hang Tag
(pages 30–33).

Coconut Curry Simmer Sauce

Make this and give away two jars as gifts, and keep two
jars on hand for a quick and tasty dinner.

2 tablespoons (30 ml) olive oil

2 tablespoons (30 g) minced garlic

3 ½ cups (823 ml) full-fat coconut milk

3 tablespoons (15 g) ground coriander

3 tablespoons (20 g) turmeric

2 tablespoons (16 g) chili powder

1 tablespoon (6 g) ground cumin

1 tablespoon (6 g) ground black pepper

1 teaspoon sea salt

¾ teaspoon ground cinnamon

¾ teaspoon fennel seed

¼ teaspoon red pepper flakes

¼ teaspoon ground cloves

¼ teaspoon ground cardamom

¼ cup (60 ml) lime juice

2 tablespoons (16 g) cornstarch mixed
with ¼ cup (60 ml) water to make
a slurry

For Canning:

4 (8-ounce, or 235 ml) jars

4 rings and lids

Other "Materials Needed," page 137

Heat the olive oil in a pot over medium heat. Add the garlic and
sauté until fragrant, about 3 to 5 minutes. Add the coconut milk
and stir to combine.

Stir in the spices and bring to a boil over medium-high. Reduce
the heat to a simmer and simmer for 15 minutes.

Stir in the lime juice, then add the cornstarch slurry and stir to
thicken.

Follow canning instructions as outlined in "Canning Basics"
on pages 136–139. Processing time is 30 minutes. Any jars that
did not seal need to be stored in the refrigerator and used within
a week. Refrigerate after opening.

YIELD: 4 (8-ounce, or 235 ml) jars

Gift It!

Affix a pretty handwritten
Label (pages 30–31) that reads:
"Use this delicious Coconut
Curry Simmer Sauce to liven
up vegetables, put a new spin
on rice, simmer with tofu, or
sauté with any of your favorite
proteins. Refrigerate after
opening."

Buffalo
Hot Sauce

Buffalo Hot Sauce

What most people don't know is that Buffalo sauce is really easy to make.
It is simply one part melted butter mixed with one part hot pepper sauce—Frank's on the
East Coast, Tabasco on the West. That really is it. But, you know we DIY-type folks
like to take it to the next level, by making our own hot sauce first!

For Hot Pepper Sauce:

1 pound (454 g) fresh red jalapeños
  or other spicy red pepper

2 tablespoons (30 ml) olive oil

1 cup (235 ml) distilled white vinegar

2 teaspoons sea salt

For Buffalo Hot Sauce:

2 cups (470 ml) hot pepper sauce,
  store-bought or homemade
  (see recipe above)

2 cups (448 g) nondairy butter

1 tablespoon (15 g) minced garlic

1 teaspoon red pepper flakes, for extra
  heat (optional)

For Canning:

4 (8-ounce, or 235 ml) jars

4 rings and lids

Other "Materials Needed," page 137

To make the hot pepper sauce: Preheat the oven to
400°F (200°C, or gas mark 6). Line a rimmed baking sheet with
aluminum foil.

In a bowl, toss the jalapeños in the olive oil to coat. Arrange the
peppers in a single layer on the prepared baking sheet and roast
for 1 hour, or until browned and charred.

Remove from the oven and allow to cool completely. Remove
and discard the stems.

Transfer the roasted peppers, and all of the juices that may be
hanging out on the foil, to a food processor. Purée.

Strain into a bowl through a fine-mesh sieve, pressing with the
back of a wooden spoon, to get as much of the pulp as possible.
Add the vinegar and salt and stir to combine.

If at this point you want to bottle your own hot sauce, proceed
to the canning instructions.

To make the Buffalo sauce: Combine the hot sauce,
butter, garlic, and red pepper flakes (if using) in a pot and heat
over medium heat until the butter is completely melted.

Follow canning instructions as outlined in "Canning Basics"
on pages 136–139. Processing time is 20 minutes. Any jars that
did not seal need to be stored in the refrigerator and used within
a week. Refrigerate after opening.

YIELD: 4 (8-ounce, or 235 ml) jars

Gift It!

Don't forget to tie on a handwritten Hang Tags
(pages 30–33) with a pretty ribbon or twine.

Sweet Whiskey Barbecue Sauce

This sweet and tangy barbecue sauce can do battle against any store-bought version. I might even venture to say that whoever receives this as a gift will tell you it's the best barbecue sauce they've ever had. What makes it so special? You made it!

¼ cup (60 ml) olive oil

1 medium yellow onion, roughly chopped

6 to 8 cloves garlic, minced

2 (15-ounce, or 425 g each) cans tomato sauce

¼ cup (60 ml) vegan Worcestershire sauce

½ cup (160 g) grape jelly

1 cup (220 g) firmly packed brown sugar

1 tablespoon (15 g) sriracha

½ cup (120 ml) whiskey

2 tablespoons (30 ml) liquid smoke

¼ cup (60 g) Dijon mustard

Salt and pepper to taste

For Canning:

6 (8-ounce, or 235 ml) jars

6 rings and lids

Other "Materials Needed," page 137

Heat the oil in a medium-size pot over medium-high heat. Add the onion and garlic and sauté for about 5 minutes, until fragrant and translucent.

Add the tomato sauce, Worcestershire, grape jelly, brown sugar, sriracha, whiskey, liquid smoke, mustard, salt, and pepper and stir to combine. Bring to a boil, reduce the heat to low, cover, and simmer for 30 minutes, until thick and fragrant.

If desired, use an immersion blender or carefully transfer to a tabletop blender and purée until smooth. (Personally, I like a few chunky pieces of onion and garlic!)

Follow canning instructions as outlined in "Canning Basics" on pages 136–139. Processing time is 15 minutes. Any jars that did not seal need to be stored in the refrigerator and used within a week. Refrigerate after opening.

YIELD: 6 (8-ounce, or 235 ml) jars

Gift It!

Don't forget to tie on a handwritten Hang Tag (pages 30–33) with a pretty ribbon or twine.

Salted Caramel Sauce

Yummy caramel sauce to pour over ice cream . . . or eat with a spoon!

2 cups (470 ml) light corn syrup

4 cups (800 g) evaporated cane juice or granulated sugar

1 cup (224 g) nondairy butter, cubed

¼ cup (32 g) cornstarch

2 cups (470 ml) soy or other nondairy milk

1 tablespoon (15 ml) vanilla extract

1 teaspoon fine sea salt

For Canning:

7 (8-ounce, or 235 ml) jars

7 lids and rings

Other "Materials Needed," page 137

In a deep pot, melt the corn syrup and evaporated cane juice over medium heat, stirring often. It will begin to bubble and turn golden amber in color.

Add the butter cubes and stir until melted.

Mix the cornstarch into the milk to make a slurry. Continue to stir as you add the milk and cornstarch slurry. The mixture will bubble and froth as you add the milk. Remove from the heat and stir until completely smooth and silky. Stir in the vanilla and salt.

Follow canning instructions as outlined in "Canning Basics" on pages 136–139. Processing time is 15 minutes. Any jars that did not seal need to be stored in the refrigerator and used within a week. Refrigerate after opening.

YIELD: 7 (8-ounce, or 235 ml) jars

Red Wine Hot Fudge Sauce

Hot fudge sauce for grown-ups! Hooray!

4 cups (700 g) vegan semisweet chocolate chips

2 cups (470 ml) Cabernet Sauvignon or your favorite wed wine

2 cups (400 g) sugar

¼ cup (56 g) nondairy butter

½ cup (64 g) cornstarch mixed with ¼ cup (60 ml) soy milk to make a slurry

2 tablespoons (30 ml) vanilla extract

4 teaspoons (20 ml) almond extract

For Canning:

6 (8-ounce, or 235 ml) jars

6 rings and lids

Other "Materials Needed," page 137

Combine the chocolate chips, wine, sugar, and butter in a saucepan and bring to a boil over medium heat. Boil for 3 minutes, stirring constantly.

Add the cornstarch slurry and stir until thickened.

Remove from the heat and continue to stir. Add the vanilla and almond extracts and keep stirring until shiny and smooth.

Follow canning instructions as outlined in "Canning Basics" on pages 136–139. Processing time is 15 minutes. Any jars that did not seal need to be stored in the refrigerator and used within a week. Refrigerate after opening.

YIELD: 6 (8-ounce, or 235 ml) jars

Chapter 6

Last Call!

Homemade Liqueurs, Infusions, Mixers, and More

Homemade liquor gifts. Now don't worry, we ain't talkin' moonshine here. More like infused vodkas, spiced rums, *muy caliente* tequilas, and sweet liqueurs. Also included are bar mixes, such as simple syrups, and cocktail mixers.

There are a lot of recipes that call for spirits in this chapter, and many people are unsure of whether their spirits are vegan or not—and guess what? Sometimes they're not! Animal-derived ingredients such as isinglass, egg whites, dairy, and honey can sometimes find their way into our adult beverages. Since most alcoholic beverages do not contain ingredient labels, it's hard to tell. I recommend visiting the fabulous website Barnivore. com. They have done all of the hard work for us, and compiled a comprehensive list of alcohols, from beers and wines to distilled spirits, with information on whether they are vegan-friendly.

Strawberry
Simple Syrup

handmade
with love!

keep refrigerated

Simple Syrups

Simple syrups can be used to make cocktails, sweeten teas, and even brush on cakes before frosting to add moisture. A plain simple syrup can be made using equal parts sugar and water. The following are three of my favorite flavored syrups.

Strawberry Simple Syrup

4 cups (940 g) water

16 ounces (448 g) frozen strawberries

4 cups (800 g) evaporated cane juice or granulated sugar

Orange Simple Syrup

4 cups (940 g) water

2 oranges, sliced with skin on

4 cups (800 g) evaporated cane juice or granulated sugar

Vanilla Simple Syrup

4 cups (940 g) water

1 (4-inch, or 10 cm) vanilla bean, split lengthwise

4 cups (800 g) evaporated cane juice or granulated sugar

In a saucepot, bring the water and strawberries, or oranges, or vanilla bean to a boil over high heat. Boil for 5 minutes, crushing the fruit to release all of its goodness.

Reduce the heat to low and add the sugar. Stir until the sugar is completely dissolved.

Remove from the heat and allow to cool completely.

Strain out the solids, and pour into jars or bottles.

Keep refrigerated.

YIELD: Each recipe yields 6 cups (1.4 L)

Gift It!

Use a pretty ribbon or twine to attach the recipe card (page 168). Don't forget to add your own handwritten Label (pages 30–31) with a note to keep the syrup refrigerated.

Grenadine

Probably the most misdiagnosed flavor of all time. Yes, it's made from pomegranate, not cherry! It is the essential ingredient in classic mocktails such as the Shirley Temple or the Roy Rogers, but don't forget its importance in the popular Tequila Sunrise or less popular Queen Mary (grenadine mixed with beer!).

4 cups (940 ml) 100% pomegranate juice

4 cups (800 g) evaporated cane juice or granulated sugar

In a saucepot, bring the juice to a boil over medium-high heat. Reduce the heat to low and add the sugar. Stir until the sugar is completely dissolved. Remove from the heat and allow to cool completely.

Package in jars or bottles. Keep refrigerated.

YIELD: 6 cups (1.4 L)

Cocktail Ideas for Simple Syrups and Grenadine

Pink Sunrise
- 2 parts orange juice
- 1 part Strawberry Simple Syrup or Grenadine
- 1 part vodka

Orange Pop
- 2 parts club soda
- 1 part Orange Simple Syrup
- 1 part whiskey

Iced Vani-Latte
- 1 part cold espresso
- 1 part Vanilla Simple Syrup
- 1 part coconut (or other nondairy) milk
- 1 part lite rum

Pour over ice and stir.
Yield: 1 serving each

★ | $

Sweet and Sour Mix

Sweet and sour mix is an essential ingredient for many classic cocktails, such as the Whiskey Sour. The problem is that the stuff you buy at the store is a terrible blend of artificial colors, flavors, and high-fructose corn syrup. It's really easy to make up a batch, and it is a great host or hostess gift.

3 lemons, sliced

3 limes, sliced

2 cups (400 g) evaporated cane juice or granulated sugar

4 cups (940 ml) water

½ cup (120 ml) lemon juice

½ cup (120 ml) lime juice

Add the lemons, limes, sugar, and water to a pot. Bring to a boil over medium-high heat, reduce the heat to a simmer, and simmer for 20 minutes. Stir in the lemon and lime juices.

Remove from the heat. Strain out the solids. (Reserve a slice of lime and a slice of lemon to add to each bottle of mix, if for no other reason than it looks nice!)

Allow to cool completely. Package in bottles or mason jars. Refrigerate after opening.

YIELD: 4 cups (940 ml)

Sweet and Sour Mix Cocktail Ideas

Classic Whiskey Sour
- 2 ounces (60 ml) whiskey
- 1 ounce (30 ml) Sweet and Sour Mix
- Lime wedge, for garnish

Mix and pour over ice. Garnish with a wedge of lime.

Yield: 1 serving

Tropical Iced Tea
- 2 ounces (60 ml) pineapple juice
- 2 ounces (60 ml) dark rum
- 2 ounces (60 ml) vodka
- 2 ounces (60 ml) Sweet and Sour Mix
- Pineapple wedge, for garnish

Add to a cocktail shaker with ice, shake, and pour into a tall glass. Serve garnished with a wedge of pineapple.

Yield: 1 serving

Vegameister

Gramma Nan taught me how to make homemade Kahlva, and now
I shall teach y'all how to make Vegameister, my homemade version of Jägermeister.

16 whole star anise

1 cup (235 ml) water

2 cups (400 g) evaporated cane
juice or granulated sugar

4 cups (940 ml) vodka

1 (4-inch, or 10 cm) vanilla
bean, split lengthwise

4 slices (about 1 ounce, or 28
g) fresh ginger (unpeeled
is fine)

4 whole black peppercorns

2 whole cloves

1 teaspoon whole fennel seed

½ teaspoon food-grade dried
lavender flowers

In a saucepot, bring the star anise and water to a boil over high heat. Boil for 5 minutes.

Add the evaporated cane juice and stir until completely dissolved. Remove from the heat and allow to cool completely.

Add the vodka, vanilla bean, ginger, peppercorns, cloves, fennel, and lavender and stir to combine. Pour into a jar or container with a tight-fitting lid.

Allow to sit for 7 days, giving it a shake every day. Strain out the solids and pour into bottles, then seal.

YIELD: 6 cups (1.4 L)

Vegameister

This intensely flavored sweet liqueur is rich with the flavor of black licorice. Just like its commercial counterpart, it makes a great shot! Here are some other ways to enjoy it:

Moloko
Mix equal parts coconut milk and Vegameister and shoot it!

Fiery Demon
Mix equal parts cinnamon schnapps and Vegameister and shoot it!

Drunken Fuzzy Navel
Mix equal parts peach schnapps, orange juice, and Vegameister and shoot it!

Gift It!

Pour into pretty bottles or mason jars and attach the recipe card at right.

Gramma Nan's Homemade Kahlúa

This recipe came from my Gramma Nan. How cool is that?
It takes at least thirty days for this to fully develop,
but it's worth the wait.

4 cups (800 g) sugar

2 ounces (56 g) instant coffee crystals

2 cups (470 ml) boiling water

2 cups (470 ml) vodka

½ vanilla bean per bottle

In a heat-safe bowl, mix the sugar and instant coffee crystals together. Add the boiling water and stir until completely dissolved.

Cool completely. Add the vodka stir to combine, and pour into bottles. Add ½ vanilla bean to each bottle. Cap and date. Let stand for at least 30 days before opening.

YIELD: 8 cups (2 L)

Gift It!

Dip the caps (or corks) into melted wax to seal the bottles. Tie on the recipe card at right.

Gramma Nan's Homemade Kahlúa

There are many classic cocktails that call for Kahlúa. Here are two of my favorite ways to enjoy it.

Gramma Nan's and Cream
Mix equal parts Gramma Nan's and nondairy vanilla creamer and pour over ice.

Gramma Nan's and Coffee
Add 2 ounces (30 ml) Gramma Nan's to a cup of coffee for a pick-me-up with a kick!

Bloody Mary Mix

This is a great host or hostess gift, but it does require refrigeration, so keep that in mind!

3 cups (705 ml) tomato juice

¼ cup (60 ml) lemon juice

¼ cup (60 ml) lime juice

2 tablespoons (30 ml) vegan Worcestershire sauce

1 tablespoon (7 g) celery salt

1 teaspoon ground black pepper

¼ teaspoon cayenne pepper (more or less according to taste)

¼ teaspoon red pepper flakes (more or less according to taste)

Mix all the ingredients together and pour into a bottle or jar.

YIELD: 4 cups (1 L)

Bloody Mary Mix

Keep refrigerated.

To Serve:
Fill a pint glass with ice. Add 2 ounces (60 ml) vodka, and top off with Bloody Mary Mix. Pour into a shaker and shake.

Salt the rim of a glass with celery salt. Pour the shaken Bloody Mary into the glass.

Garnish with a celery stalk, a green olive, a clove of garlic, and a sprinkle of freshly cracked pepper.

Yield: 1 serving

Gift It!
Pour into a decorative bottle and affix the recipe card shown at right.

★ | $$

Muy Caliente Tequila con Pimienta

This drink, as its name suggests, is super-hot, and the perfect gift for that special spicy someone.

2 serrano chiles (habanero, if you dare!), chopped (leave in seeds for an extra spicy infusion)

1 lime, sliced

1 fresh mango, peeled, pitted, and diced

3 cloves garlic, cut in half

1 sprig fresh tarragon

3 cups (705 ml) silver or blanco tequila

Add all the ingredients to a glass container with a tight-fitting lid. Store in a cool, dry place for 48 to 72 hours. The longer you steep it, the spicier it will be. Strain out the solids, pour into a bottle and seal.

YIELD: 3 cups (705 ml)

Gift It!

Look for a cool bottle at import stores or thrift shops. If you want a really cool effect, melt some food-grade paraffin wax (available in the canning section of your supermarket) and dip the capped bottle into it to seal. Dip once, allow to cool, dip again, and repeat until the desired thickness and appearance is achieved. Tie the recipe card at right to the neck of the bottle with hemp or jute twine.

Jalapeño-Lime Orangarita

- 1 tablespoon (1 g) fresh cilantro
- 2 or 3 slices fresh jalapeño, divided
- 2 ounces (60 ml) Muy Caliente Tequila con Pimienta
- 4 ounces (120 ml) freshly squeezed orange juice
- Juice of ½ lime
- 1 tablespoon (15 ml) agave nectar
- Coarse sea salt

Muddle the cilantro and 1 or 2 slices of the jalapeño (reserving 1 slice for garnish) in the bottom of a glass. To a cocktail shaker, add the muddled cilantro and jalapeño, ice, infused tequila, orange juice, lime juice, and agave. Shake. Rim a glass with coarse salt. Pour the drink into the glass and add a slice of jalapeño to the rim as a garnish.

Yield: 1 serving

Irish Crème

I won't bore you with tales of when I hit many a wall drinking Bailey's over ice in my pregan (before I was a vegan) days. Only recently have I been able to relive my youth with this homemade vegan version. To be true to its roots, try to use Irish whiskey. If you use 80-proof (40 percent alcohol by volume) whiskey, your final product will be 10 percent alcohol by volume. Not quite as stiff as a cocktail, but definitely stronger than a beer. I like mine in coffee or over ice.

- **2 cups (470 ml) vanilla soy or coconut creamer, such as Silk or So Delicious**
- **1 cup (200 g) evaporated cane juice or granulated sugar**
- **1 cup (235 ml) strongly brewed coffee**
- **1 tablespoon (5 g) cocoa powder**
- **1 tablespoon (15 ml) vanilla extract**
- **1 cup (235 ml) Irish whiskey**

Add the creamer, evaporated cane juice, coffee, and cocoa powder to a saucepot. Heat over medium heat until the sugar and cocoa have completely dissolved.

Remove from the heat. Allow to cool completely. Stir in the vanilla and whiskey.

Pour into bottles and seal. Keep refrigerated.

YIELD: 4 cups (1 L)

Gift It!

Add your own handwritten Label (pages 30–31) with a note to enjoy as is or mixed with a cup of coffee topped with nondairy whipped topping.

Holiday Spiced Rum

This is some serious stuff. Last Christmas, I packaged this up in mason jars and made handwritten tags that read "Christmas Moonshine," and the men in my family couldn't have been happier. It's sometimes hard to find homemade gifts that appeal to men. Liquor fits that bill quite nicely.

2 whole cinnamon sticks

10 whole cloves

10 whole allspice berries

1 (4-inch, or 10 cm) vanilla bean, split lengthwise

1 teaspoon dried orange peel

½ teaspoon whole fennel seed

¼ teaspoon ground nutmeg

¼ teaspoon ground ginger

2 cups (470 ml) clear rum

Add all the spices to a container with a tight-fitting lid. Pour the rum over the spices and seal the container. Shake to mix.

Let sit for 5 days, shaking once each day, before straining out all of the solids through a sieve lined with cheesecloth to get as many of the fine particles as possible. Pour into a bottle and seal.

YIELD: 2 cups (470 ml)

Gift It!

This looks really great packaged up in mason jars, with some twine and a couple of whole cinnamon sticks tied around the top. Be sure to attach the recipe card at right.

Spiked Holiday Cider

- 2 ounces (60 ml) Holiday Spiced Rum
- 2 ounces (60 ml) cinnamon schnapps
- 4 ounces (120 ml) hot apple cider
- Cinnamon stick, for garnish

Add the rum and schnapps to a coffee mug. Stir in the hot apple cider. Serve with a cinnamon stick for garnish.

Yield: 1 serving

Raspberry Lime Gin

So this just might be my new favorite adult beverage!
I've been enjoying it straight over ice, but it also tastes fantastic mixed
with club soda to make a Sweet Raspberry Lime Rickey. And that color!
All natural from the berries. Mother Nature is so awesome, isn't she?

1 ½ cups (170 g) **fresh raspberries**

2 **limes, sliced**

2 cups (400 g) **evaporated cane juice or
granulated sugar**

2 cups (470 ml) **water**

½ cup (120 ml) **lime juice**

4 cups (940 ml) **gin**

Add the berries, lime slices, evaporated cane juice, and water to a
pot and stir to combine. Bring to a boil over medium-high heat,
reduce the heat to a simmer, cover, and simmer for 1 hour.

Set aside and allow to cool completely. Stir in the lime juice
and gin.

Strain out the solids, pour into bottles, seal, and attach the
recipe card below.

YIELD: 6 cups (1.4 L)

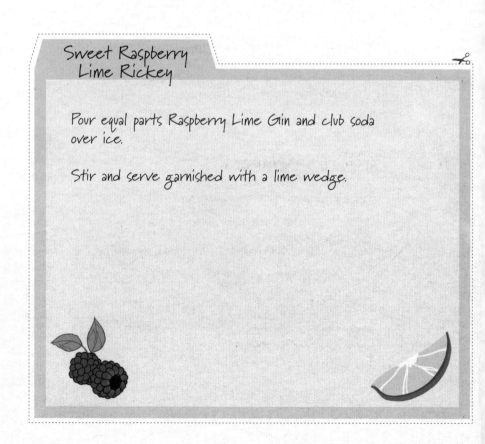

Sweet Raspberry Lime Rickey

Pour equal parts Raspberry Lime Gin and club soda
over ice.

Stir and serve garnished with a lime wedge.

Eggless Wassail

Traditional wassail contains a lot of eggs, which are beaten into stiff peaks, and then some is folded into the mixture and the rest is floated on top like foam. I don't know about you guys, but vegan or not, that just sounds nasty. The coconut milk here stands in for the eggs, and it actually does separate from the rest of the mix and float on top. Remember to serve it hot!

4 red apples

¼ cup (55 g) firmly packed brown sugar

20 whole cloves

1 orange

4 cups (940 ml) apple juice

2 cinnamon sticks

1 whole star anise

10 allspice berries

½ teaspoon ground ginger

¼ teaspoon ground nutmeg

2 cups (470 ml) full-fat coconut milk

2 cups (470 ml) brandy

Preheat the oven to 350°F (180°C, or gas mark 4). Line a rimmed baking sheet with aluminum foil.

Scoop out the top of each apple with a melon baller and stuff about 1 tablespoon (14 g) brown sugar into each apple. Place on the baking sheet.

Poke the whole cloves into the orange. Place on the baking sheet. Bake for 1 hour.

Combine the apple juice, cinnamon sticks, anise, allspice, ginger, and nutmeg in a pot with a lid.

Remove the baked apples and orange from the oven. Cut the orange in half. Transfer fruit to the pot. Bring to a boil over high heat, reduce the heat to a simmer, cover, and simmer for 1 hour.

Remove from the heat. Stir in the coconut milk and brandy, and mix until well combined.

Strain out the solids and pour into jars or bottles.

The coconut milk will separate and float to the top. That's okay. Just shake well before serving.

This tastes best served hot. Keep refrigerated.

YIELD: 6 cups (1.4 L)

Gift It!

Tie on a handwritten Hang Tag (pages 30–33) with a note that reads "Best served hot! Keep refrigerated until ready to use."

Vanilla
Mint
Vodka

Vanilla Mint Vodka

★ | $$

This is a snap to make. And, depending on how long you let it steep, you can make it a mellow vanilla mint or a deep vanilla that will make even an anti-vodka person fall in love. This recipe is for 2 cups (470 ml). I like to make bigger batches and make lots of gifts at a time. Double, triple, or quadruple the recipe as needed.

2 cups (470 ml) vodka

1 vanilla bean, split lengthwise

10 mint leaves

Add all the ingredients to a jar or bottle with a tight-fitting lid and shake. Allow to steep for 24 hours up to 5 full days, until the desired flavor is achieved, shaking a couple of times a day. I like to steal a spoonful each day to test it . . . for research purposes, of course! Strain out the solids, then pour into a bottle and seal.

YIELD: 2 cups (470 ml)

Gift It!

Look for a cool bottle at import stores or thrift shops. If you want a really cool effect, melt some food-grade paraffin wax (available in the canning section of your supermarket) and dip the capped bottle into it to seal. Dip once, allow to cool, dip again, and repeat until the desired thickness and appearance are achieved. Tie the recipe card at right to the neck of the bottle with hemp or jute twine.

Candy Cane Martini

- 2 ounces (30 ml) Vanilla Mint Vodka
- 1 ounce (15 ml) peppermint schnapps
- 1 ounce (15 ml) nondairy vanilla creamer, such as Silk or So Delicious
- 1 ounce (15 ml) grenadine
- Sugar, for rimming the martini glass
- Mint leaves and a candy cane or peppermint stick, for garnish

To a cocktail shaker, add the vodka, schnapps, creamer, grenadine, and ice. Shake to mix. Rim a martini glass with sugar. Pour the cocktail into the glass, and add the mint leaves and candy cane as a garnish.

Yield: 1 serving

GIN-ger Snap

This stuff is no joke. It's made with gin and definitely has a snap!

2 ½ ounces (70 g) fresh ginger, sliced (unpeeled is fine)

2 cinnamon sticks

1 teaspoon dried orange peel

4 cups (940 ml) gin

Add the ginger, cinnamon sticks, and orange peel to a container with a tight-fitting lid. Pour in the gin, seal, give it a good shake, and let it sit for 1 full week, shaking once daily.

Strain out the solids (I like to leave in the cinnamon sticks), pour into bottles and seal.

YIELD: 4 cups (940 ml)

GIN-ger Snap Cocktails

Hot Cranberry Ginger Tea
- 4 ounces (120 ml) hot brewed black tea (Earl Grey is fabulous here!)
- 2 ounces (60 ml) cranberry juice
- 2 ounces (60 ml) GIN-ger Snap
- Drizzle of agave nectar

Stir all the ingredients together and serve hot.

Yield: 1 serving

Stiff Ginger Ale
- 4 ounces (120 ml) club soda
- 2 ounces (60 ml) GIN-ger Snap
- 2 ounces (60 ml) lemon-lime soda

Stir all the ingredients together and pour over ice. Garnish with a lemon wedge.

Yield: 1 serving

Gift It!
Package in pretty bottles or mason jars, affix a Label (pages 30–31) to the bottle, and attach the recipe card at right.

Resources

The majority of the ingredients in this book are readily available at your local supermarket or health food store. For those who can't get their hands on certain ingredients in their neck of the woods, I highly recommend the following online retailers.

Ball and Kerr

Daleville, Indiana • www.freshpreserving.com • All the canning tools you will ever need. The site also offers lots of information on home canning and recipes for preserves.

Food Fight! Grocery

Portland, Oregon • www.foodfightgrocery.com • Everything vegan under the sun. From candy bars and vegan marshmallows, to nutritional yeast and TVP. You can also pick up a "What kind of asshole eats a lamb?" T-shirt or reusable grocery tote designed by my friend and amazing illustrator Kurt Halsey.

The Jar Store

Bloomfield, Connecticut • www.jarstore.com • Any kind of jar you can think of for canning and crafting—square, round, tall, short, you name it.

Penzeys Spices

Locations throughout the United States • www.penzeys.com • Excellent prices and a huge variety of herbs and spices. They also sell high-quality empty jars for bulk or custom spice blends for as little as $1.35!

Vegan Essentials

Milwaukee, Wisconsin • www.veganessentials.com • Everything they sell is vegan: shoes, food, books, clothing, body care products, supplements—all of the vegan essentials!

Vegan Etsy

www.etsy.com/people/VeganEtsy • A team of vegans who run shops on Etsy, the world's handmade marketplace. These talented folks are dedicated to promoting not only a DIY ethic but a DIY vegan ethic as well. Throughout the pages of this book, you will see props used in the photos that were purchased from them.

Weck

www.weckjars.com • A different type of home canning system that uses rubber rings and clamps instead of lids and rings. The jars are beautiful, if a little more pricey than those from Ball or Kerr.

Acknowledgments

I would like to extend a gracious and heartfelt thank-you to Amanda Waddell, who has now helped me get through five cookbooks! Her hard work, creativity, faith, and patience have made all of my experiences with her nothing short of spectacular. I would also like to offer great thanks to Jennifer Grady, Meghan Sniegoski, Betsy Gammons, Kathryn Ahlin, and Karen Levy, without whom this book would not have been possible.

A very special appreciation goes out to the amazing testers who kept me in line throughout the whole process. Kelly Cavalier, you are an amazing woman! I think you tested almost every recipe in the book. Your thorough and honest feedback was fantastic.

Anna Holt (and sons!), Kelly Williams, Jared Bigman, Stephanie Stanesby, David Cockerham, Agnes Martin, Adrienne Lowe, Christy Beauregard, Megan Storms, Megan Hall, Kele Usilton, Kala Patterson, Ted Lai, Monika Caruso, and Rebekah Reid . . . thank you guys so much!

Mommy, if it weren't for you, entire sections of this book could not have happened. I am so lucky to have you as my mom, and a sincere thanks for all of your help with this book. Do you think anyone noticed your hands in that one picture on the step-by-step photos? Whoops! I guess they'll notice now!

Dan, thanks for once again giving up on keeping a tidy house as ribbons, papers, glue, jars, and jellies got stacked and strewn about on every possible flat surface in our tiny little house. I love you more than ever!

And finally, I want to appreciate two wonderfully talented people; if it weren't for them, this would be a very boring book to look at. Celine, your photos, as always, bring to life what otherwise would just be words on a page. I am grateful for knowing you and ever impressed by your ability to shoot such amazing pictures. Kurt, you amaze me with your adorable drawings, paintings, and illustrations. How did I get so lucky to have you as a friend, and now a brother? Thanks for taking on this challenge and putting your heart into every brushstroke.

About the Author

I am Joni Marie Newman. I am just a regular gal who loves to cook and bake—especially for friends and family. Self-taught, and still learning, I spend most of my spare time in the kitchen. When I am not in the kitchen, I really enjoy knitting, painting, wasting endless hours on the Internet, hiking with my husband and the girls, traveling, reading, and most of the other stuff regular gals enjoy. I currently reside in Orange County, California, but before you go all Real Housewives of Orange County on me, let me tell you that I live in a small cottage, with my three rescue mutts, my very handsome cat, and my extremely delicious husband, in one of the last rural towns in Southern California. It is in this cottage that I create delicious and cruelty-free delicacies for the world to enjoy. Through my food, I hope to help people understand that it is not necessary to murder or torture another living creature in order to have a tasty supper. I can be reached through my website at www.justthefood.com or on twitter @jonimarienewman.

Index